D0487578

BACK FROM THE BRINK

GUY MOUNTFORT

Back from the Brink
Successes in Wildlife Conservation

Foreword by
SIR PETER SCOTT
C.B.E., D.S.C., LL.D.

Hutchinson of London

Hutchinson & Co (Publishers) Ltd
3 Fitzroy Square, London W1

London Melbourne Sydney Auckland
Wellington Johannesburg and agencies
throughout the world

First published 1978
© Guy Mountfort 1978

Set in Monotype Baskerville

Printed in Great Britain by The Anchor Press Ltd
and bound by Wm Brendon & Son Ltd
both of Tiptree, Essex

ISBN 0 09 132710 5

For Anna, Paul, Oliver and Stephen,
who one day will know why Grandpa
thought the protection of wildlife
so important for their future.

Contents

Illustrations

Foreword

by Sir Peter Scott
C.B.E., D.S.C., LL.D.

Chairman of the World Wildlife Fund

Nowadays most people realize how acute the pressure is on the natural environment. Ever more relentlessly we threaten the animals and plants and the 'ecological webs' which bind them together with the climate, soil and water into those healthy ecosystems which for centuries man has characterized by the word 'Nature'. Our ignorance of nature, our apathy, our greed, our avarice and our increasing numbers have already exterminated or severely depleted the populations of many living organisms – our fellow crew-members on 'Spaceship Earth'. Today's animal and plant species are the current end-product of thirty million centuries of evolution since life began on the planet. Species have evolved and become extinct since the beginning of those three thousand million years, but now the activities of man seem to have increased the rate of extinction by a factor of at least four, and some have indicated a factor of more than ten. So the marvellous diversity of the living world is beginning to diminish. Some living forms may be 'booked for extinction' even without our destructive intervention. But man is a part of nature, a predatory primate with a unique intelligence which has developed in us a sense of right and wrong – of responsibility for our actions. This conscience has in turn led to the evolution of an ethic of conservation.

The irrevocability of the extinction of any living form capable of self-perpetuation is something which touches that conscience. In the view of most people who stop to think about it, even the accidental extermination of a species by mankind is inexcusable. The prevention of species extinction has been and still is the simple aim of the Survival Service Commission of the International Union for Conservation of Nature and a prime concern of the World Wildlife Fund. In this book the author, who was very closely associated with the establishment of the WWF in 1961, describes some of the successful conservation projects that have been undertaken since that time. Assuring the survival of a single species may seem a limited success when so many are in danger, yet even the examples here described amount in aggregate to a significant achievement. Often, too, the effort to save a species requires the saving of its habitat, and this in turn may safeguard many other species of animals and plants which are a part of the same ecosystem. Operation Tiger – the brilliant brain child of Guy Mountfort – has led to the establishment of special reserves which have helped to save many other threatened plants and animals as well as the tiger. A host of much smaller and less ambitious projects has had the same effect.

Conservation of natural environment in the long term will depend not only on the success of all those projects which may seem small in themselves, but also on the capacity of mankind to come to terms with the causal factors which make nature conservation so necessary and urgent at the moment – the problems of human population increase, of high technology agriculture, of industrialization and urbanization, of pollution, of misuse and waste of resources and energy, of famine and of poverty. If solutions to these problems are found then lasting conservation of nature may yet be achieved, but it cannot be dealt with in isolation from the human condition.

Meanwhile, the time is appropriate to record such successes as have been won. In *Back from the Brink* Guy Mountfort has skilfully brought these specific stories together and related them to the overall picture of the natural environment in this last quarter of the twentieth century. I am delighted to be associated with such a well-documented account of the conservation achievements of recent years in the vital field of endangered species and their habitats.

Author's preface

Looking back on the growth of the conservation movement, I suppose Rachel Carson's *Silent Spring*, published in 1962, was the first book which really aroused people of many nations to an awareness of the tragedies which are overtaking the natural world. Since then, of course, there has been a torrent of books in a similar vein, though very few achieved such an impact. Their sheer mass, however, supported by innumerable television documentaries, has resulted in a very high degree of public interest in conservation. The press and broadcasting media were quick to recognize this and to cater for it by opening their doors to specialists who could interpret the sometimes unfamiliar language of scientific conservationists. Even politicians, who as a rule prefer to follow rather than lead any new development in public opinion, responded in many countries by creating new ministries for the protection of the environment and wildlife.

Unfortunately, while it is obviously important that the public should understand the extent to which the world is being despoiled by pollution and the destruction of natural resources, the great majority of books on the subject paint a picture of unrelieved gloom. The average reader can be forgiven for putting them down with a sigh, feeling that the problems are now so overpowering that very little can be done about them. Everyone now knows that our coasts, rivers and off-shore waters are heavily polluted; that overcrowded Britain is losing 200 acres of countryside under bricks or concrete each day; that wildlife is disappearing. The global situation is also now painfully familiar and equally depressing. The human population will double in thirty years and already one-third of it lives at or below bare subsistence level. Most of us know that in the last ten years food production has decreased, while the population has increased by 700 millions. The litany of impending disaster for mankind is hard to escape and the writers of such books cannot be surprised if they are dubbed the prophets of doom.

It is against this dismal background that I have been tempted to write yet another book about conservation. But this time with a difference. It is about successes rather than problems.

Perhaps it will cheer the despondent to be reminded that conservation is making substantial if belated progress in many spheres. There are now powerful agencies of the United Nations and Council of Europe at work on all the more obvious opportunities for safeguarding the human environment and for making wiser and more equitable use of our limited natural resources. People who cause serious pollution can now be held accountable and can be severely punished. Nor can industry and aviation any longer ignore the impact of their activities on public opinion. Less harmful and more selective pesticides are being developed. Biodegradable packaging will replace the indestructible plastic bags and cartons which now disfigure the countryside. More and more areas of scenic importance are being set aside for public recreation and the number of wildlife reserves is constantly increasing throughout the world.

Here in Great Britain some notable successes have been achieved. The Smoke Abatement Act has miraculously cleansed the air in our industrial cities and particularly over London, where the lethal brown smog of earlier years has disappeared. Who could have imagined a few years ago that the nearly lifeless River Thames would now be so purified that ninety-one species of fish live safely in its tidal reaches? Or that the general public and the press and television would give immediate support to the creation of mini-reserves for the protection of obscure species of bats, or, even more remarkably, rare spiders? There are now more than 1000 nature reserves in this country.

Co-operation between nations in the interests of wildlife is another encouraging sign. For example, all the nations within the range of the polar bear have agreed to prevent its extinction by excessive hunting. The ratification of the Washington Convention, which banned the commercial exploitation of endangered species of animals and plants, was another big step forward. So was the international treaty to protect Antarctica from damage or exploitation. Wildlife reserves which span political frontiers are also multiplying, recent examples being the great Manas tiger reserve now shared by India and Bhutan and the new Sine Saloum wetlands reserve to be shared by Senegal and The Gambia. By no means all the conservation problems are yet being tackled, but the habit of co-operative international effort will develop further.

The catalysts in most of these recent developments have been the World Wildlife Fund and its scientific partners, the International Union for Conservation of Nature and Natural Resources (IUCN). Created in 1961 as an inter-national charitable foundation, the WWF has become, to quote a leading American magazine, a veritable 'kind of United Nations for conservation'. Through its twenty-six national organizations it had by 1977 raised nearly £20m. and had completed 1860 conservation projects in 130 different countries. As much of this expenditure was made on the basis of matching grants, that is to say of equal or greater expenditure or grants of land by recipient governments, the true value achieved by the WWF was at least twice this sum. (See Chapter 12 for a noteworthy example.) Already the new wildlife reserves it has created represent one and a half million square kilometres of protected land. Its influence with governments has become a major factor in its success. Today its panda symbol can be seen in wildlife reserves in almost every country. Part of its funds is spent on education and in this sphere the WWF Youth Service, with several hundred thousand young members in Europe, Africa and Asia, not only does useful practical conservation work but, in the western countries, also raises substantial money. The thirteen million Boy Scouts of the world have allied themselves with the WWF and adopted conservation as one of their tasks. That the WWF fills a genuine need is evident not only from the degree to which it is supported, but also from the calibre of the people who give it their voluntary services. The fact that kings and princes are numbered among them is by no means an indication of élitism, but of the universal nature of its appeal.

It would be wrong, however, to suggest that nothing was done before the World Wildlife Fund came into being. A great deal was done. As early as 1872 the magnificent Yellowstone Park, the first of its kind, was created in the State of Wyoming. In 1887 Africa's first game reserve was created in Natal, to be followed a few years later by one in the Transvaal. Africa at that period was suffering staggering losses of wildlife and was the Mecca of big-game hunters and ivory-traders of every nation. The destruction of wildlife and the creation of man-made deserts by the burning of forests had, of course, commenced long before Africa began to be 'developed' by the white man. But white farmers also regarded wild animals as competitors for their land and they slaughtered them ruthlessly. Had it not been for a few courageous and dedicated men, the list of species exterminated would have been much longer than it was.

The early pioneers of conservation in Africa were nearly all British ex-army officers who had entered the colonial administration. It is perhaps significant that the great majority of them had previously been decorated for bravery under fire, for the work they did required both courage and determination. Not all were British, however, notable exceptions being Paul Kruger in South Africa, Hermann von Wissmann in German East Africa and King Leopold II in the Belgian Congo, all of whom created wildlife reserves in the early days.

At that time there was no international body concerned with conservation and very little public interest in the subject. Nor did anyone dream that wildlife reserves in Africa would have enormous economic potential by attracting tourist revenue. The lonely pioneers had very little support. The government officials whom they had to convince were for the most part cynical and disinterested. The land developers and mineral exploiters were hostile and the native tribes jealous of any curtailment of their hunting or grazing rights. Yet the pioneers succeeded in creating a network of reserves and national parks which today are the envy of all nations. The techniques which they and American and European scientists developed for the management of wildlife provided the blueprint from which conservation throughout the world was later developed. Very few of them received any recognition for their work, but their names deserve to be enshrined.

Among the leading African figures of this epoch I would place Colonel James Stevens-Hamilton, the creator of the Kruger National Park, Captain Archie Ritchie, the doyen of African game wardens, and Captain Charles Pitman, head of the Uganda Game Department and Africa's leading expert on reptiles. Of the immediate post-World War II period I would include Colonel Mervyn Cowie, Director of the Kenya National Parks, Major Bruce Kinloch, Chief Game Warden of Uganda and later of Tanganyika and founder of the unique College of Wildlife Management at Mweka; also Major Ian Grimwood, Chief Game Warden of Kenya, David Sheldrick, pioneer of the great Tsavo National Park, and John Owen, Director of the Tanzania National Parks. There are others who equally merit inclusion. They all knew each other and were a formidable team. Some of them died in Africa; others retired with the coming of independence, or moved to other continents.

Since those early days many younger men and women from Europe and North America have justly earned fame as wildlife experts in Africa and elsewhere. Their books and films have been enjoyed by millions. But they would be the first to admit that they were building on the foundations laid by the unpublicized pioneers, to whom conservation owes an incalculable debt.

This book is concerned with examples of successful contemporary conservation. I have chosen them from among others merely because I happen to know the countries concerned and something of the problems which had to be overcome. It is not often that such obvious successes occur. Conservation is like that – some battles are won and some lost, while in the majority of cases many years must pass before any clear conclusion can be drawn.

The examples I have selected show that, given the necessary expertise and the co-operation of governments, it is sometimes possible to save animal species which have reached the very brink of extinction. So that the problems faced can be appreciated, I have sketched in the backgrounds to the case histories and described the scenes in which the work was carried out. There is no rule-of-thumb for such tasks. If some of the methods described seem unorthodox, this is a measure of the inventiveness and determination of the individuals concerned. Most of them work alone and must make their own decisions.

I hope this book may show that conservation can be an absorbing adventure as well as worth-while and that the money given to the cause by the general public is producing solid results. It may perhaps also help to answer a question often put to me: 'What do wildlife conservationists actually *do*?' The people about whom it is written are all known to me, most of them for many years. I am grateful to them for permission to describe their exploits and to make use of their reports. If there are any inaccuracies in my account of them the blame is wholly mine.

I thank the publishers of the books written by my friends, for permission to make use of some of the factual material in them. These are Messrs Macmillan (Arjan Singh's *Tiger Haven*); Messrs Collins (Barbara Harrisson's *Orang-utan* and John MacKinnon's *In Search of the Red Ape*); Messrs Allen & Unwin (Tony Beamish's *Aldabra Alone*).

Sir Peter Scott, with whom I have worked for the World Wildlife Fund on a voluntary basis for seventeen years, has been kind enough to contribute a thought-provoking foreword for which I am most grateful.

To my colleagues Peter Jackson and Dr Fritz Vollmar, who also know most of the people and places described, I am indebted for their helpful comments and advice. I am also again very grateful to my wife, who patiently puts up with my frequent absences abroad on conservation work and whose help with this book was invaluable. Finally, I thank Mrs Winifred Peck for her skill in deciphering and typing my manuscript.

I

TO CATCH A UNICORN

FROM horizon to horizon the orange-red sand of the Rub-al-Khali shimmered under the merciless sun. Even the lizards had sought shelter beneath the occasional brittle shrubs which somehow contrived to survive in the deeper depressions among the dunes. It was well named the Empty Quarter. To the north lay the Trucial States and Saudi Arabia, to the east Muscat and Oman, to the south the Aden Protectorate and in the far south-west was the Yemen. Only the brave or the foolhardy entered the Rub-al-Khali.

On the horizon a moving speck appeared. As it drew nearer, alternately elongated or flattened by the heat haze, it revealed itself as a Bedu on a camel. Shrouded in his dark robes and hooded against the sun, he was leaning forward, studying the ground intently, never losing sight of the slotted and round-toed spoor which he had patiently followed for six long days. Twice he had sighted his quarry in the far distance. Now the spoor was fresh and the end must be near. Ahead, somewhere among the rolling dunes, the trophy for which he longed would fall to his gun.

An hour later, from the crest of a high dune, he saw an outcrop of low rocks, against which the prevailing wind had piled the driven sand. The sun was over his left shoulder, which meant that a little shade would be cast on the far side of the rocks. Here, if Allah was kind, his quarry would be resting. At a quiet word the camel obediently folded its long legs and see-sawed to its knees. Sliding down from the wooden saddle, the Bedu removed it and dropped it on the sand. Pulling out his old army rifle, he slid back the bolt to make sure it was loaded and bade the camel to rise again. Driving it slowly forward with an occasional prod, he kept pace close behind it. They began a long detour, which would bring them opposite the shady side of the rocks. As they rounded the end of the outcrop, the Bedu gathered his long robe around his waist and secured it with the black *agal* cord which bound his head-cloth. Then, matching his stride to the movements of the camel's hind legs, they continued, very slowly now and stopping from time to time. Yes, praise be to Allah, there was a motionless white form standing in the shade against the rocks! It was a superb male oryx, with slender horns fully forty inches long. It was watching the solitary camel moving across its line of vision, but had not noticed the bare human legs hidden behind it. Very gently the Bedu began turning his well trained mount, a little at a time, as he raised his rifle, pressing himself flat into the hollow between its thigh and its flank. One more half-step sideways and the oryx was in full view. For a second the Bedu held his breath, transfixed by the sight of the black and white face turned so trustingly towards him, then slowly squeezed the trigger.

As the shot rang out, the oryx pitched forward, its heart's blood spurting from its dazzlingly white breast. With a cry of triumph the Bedu raced across the sand. Drawing his broad curved dagger, he cut the animal's throat as the Koran required and stood gloating over the carcass. His father and grandfather had both killed oryx in the days when they could be found even as far north as Jordan and Syria. There were none there now and he had ridden nearly 400 miles southward from Riyadh before he had found the first and only spoor. Now it would be he who would hold the elders in the great black tents spellbound with the story of his adventure.

The Bedu would have been even more impressed if he had known that the oryx he had killed was one of the last of its kind. The entire population of a once widespread species was now fewer than one hundred and declining fast. All the survivors were in this inhospitable desert between the Aden Protectorate and the Dhofar Province of Muscat.

Oryx had been hunted by the Beduin tribes since time immemorial. Little harm was done to their numbers so long as weapons were primitive. When accurate weapons from the first and second world wars began to proliferate in the Arab states, their numbers fell sharply. But it was the jeep and the big American cars fitted with sand-tyres which caused the final crash. Parties of oil-rich sheikhs, armed not only with high-powered rifles but with sub-machine guns, scoured even the remotest deserts, slaughtering everything that moved. They were not interested in trophies but in shooting. Carcasses of oryx, gazelles, hyenas, wolves, leopards, jackals and foxes were left to litter the desert where they fell. Frontiers between the various Arab states were largely unmarked and were frequently ignored. During my expedition to Jordan in 1963, hunters from Saudi Arabia and Iraq killed many gazelles and houbara bustards there, in spite of the vigilance of Jordan's fast-moving desert patrols.

The Arabian oryx is a striking animal with a white skin, black legs with white hocks and bold, black and white face-markings. It stands four feet at the shoulder and weighs about 450 pounds. Its narrowly spread horns are almost straight and fully capable of killing a leopard. It was undoubtedly an oryx seen at side view, so that the two horns looked like one, which gave rise to the Biblical myth of the unicorn, imaginary pictures of which to this day are shown with white, oryx-like skins, though usually more horse-like in form. The oryx is essentially a desert creature, drinking rarely and obtaining all the moisture it needs from roots or tubers which it digs up with its hooves. The Beduin name for it, *jawazi*, means 'he who drinks not'. The Arabian species has relations in Africa: the scimitar-horned oryx in the north, which has a rufous neck and deeply curved horns, and the beisa and gemsbok in the eastern and south-western parts. The two last mentioned resemble the Arabian but have darker skins and black flank-stripes; they are often regarded as geographical variations of the same species. Another race,

the fringe-eared oryx, which occurs from the Tana River to
Tanzania, is recognized by most authorities.

In 1961 an important meeting was held in London,
attended by experts from the Fauna Preservation Society, the
International Union for Conservation of Nature and the
World Wildlife Fund, at which the plight of the Arabian
oryx was examined. A few months previously a report had
put their population at between eighty and a hundred. The
Beduin were killing on average only five a year, the real
threat coming from motorized hunting parties from various
countries. News had just come in that one party from Saudi
Arabia had crossed the Rub-al-Khali and slaughtered forty-
eight oryx, thus wiping out half the known population.
Another such raid and the oryx would be extinct. If the
species was to be saved, there were only two possible alter-
natives: to prevent all further hunting, which was virtually
impossible in such a remote and politically sensitive area, or
to try to catch some of the survivors and breed them in
captivity for ultimate release in a fully protected area. A
decision was reached to send a properly equipped expedition
to attempt this second difficult alternative, which had been
regarded as too difficult when Dr Lee Talbot of the American
Academy of Sciences had proposed it some years previously.

'Operation Oryx' was timed for April–May 1962, when
the oryx would be driven by the heat out of the sand sea into
a region where adequately equipped vehicles could operate.
The right man was available to lead the expedition – Major
Ian Grimwood, Chief Game Warden in Kenya. I greatly
admired Ian, a lean and craggy man with a cast-iron consti-
tution, who in later years was to become famous for his
outstanding services to conservation in South America and
Asia. As deputy leader, M. A. Crouch, Assistant Adviser
in the northern deserts of the Aden Protectorate, was enlisted. Other members were Captain G. A. Shepherd of the
Armoured Car Squadron in the Federal Army of Aden,
M. H. Woodford, a veterinary surgeon from Dorset, P. W. J.
Whitehead, a former African game ranger, who would be in
charge of the catching operation, and G. K. Gracie, who

would pilot the small Piper aircraft which the East African Wildlife Society had offered to lend to the expedition. It was a strong team of specialists.

Preparations were pressed forward. In Kenya collapsible animal crates were constructed, a special catching car was built and sand-tyres fitted to the aircraft. Arrangements were made for reception pens at the Isiolo quarantine station where the oryx would be held pending shipment to their final destination. The Kenyan contingent then went off to catch some beisa oryx for practice. Meanwhile, the Fauna Preservation Society and World Wildlife Fund were raising money for the expedition and in Aden permission was being obtained from the rulers of the various states in which the expedition would have to operate.

In the midst of these preparations came two bombshells. First a report that the raiders had returned and killed another sixteen oryx. Then a second report that all the remaining oryx had been destroyed. A cable was sent immediately to Sir Charles Johnston, Governor of Aden, asking for confirmation. His reply was only mildly encouraging, to the effect that, although he could not be certain, he thought the second report might be untrue and that the expedition should continue as planned. Though deeply worried, the organizers pressed on. It was, in fact, known later that some of the oryx had escaped the raiders, though they would now be even harder to find.

On 22 March, Grimwood and Gracie set out for Aden as the advance party in an RAF Beverley transport plane, with the small Piper aircraft, the animal crates and mountains of baggage in the hold. With the generous help of the Aden Protectorate Secretary's Office and RAF Middle East Command, they were able to continue in their own plane from Aden to Riyan, 250 miles farther along the coast, where they were met by Crouch. They then drove to Mukalla, where they were installed in the Residency rest-house overlooking the Sultan's palace, to await the main party. There was plenty to keep them occupied, such as engaging servants for the expedition, building more animal crates, fetching grass and lucerne from the Wadi Hadramaut, 150 miles away, to feed the oryx, and many other details.

Problems soon arose. The Piper was grounded because the dhow bringing fuel had broken down. Stores failed to arrive from Aden. Worse still, a cable announced that the specially built Ford catching car had been refused shipment at Mombasa and no other ship was available for a month. But the RAF quickly came to the rescue and flew the car to Aden, where Grimwood went to fetch it. On the third day of the long return journey, while driving over hilly lava flows at two in the morning, the gearbox disintegrated, leaving only top gear serviceable.

Even this disaster did not deter Grimwood. There remained five days before the main party arrived, so there was time for repairs. Searching far and wide, an apparently identical gearbox was discovered in the local *suk*, but it would not fit. New gears were cut, but after being assembled and stripped down again five times, the damaged roller bearings had to be replaced by hand-made bush bearings. The gearbox finally worked, but the mechanics warned that it would have a short life. As a precaution, a reserve catching car was made by converting an old one-ton Bedford pick-up. Everything was ready on time, but ill fortune continued. Because of cancelled flights and a waterlogged airstrip, the main party arrived five days late by an unscheduled flight to Ghuraf, in the Hadhramaut, instead of reaching Mukalla. However, they arranged to join the expedition the following day when it reached Al Abr.

Early on 23 April the convoy set out from Mukalla, leaving Gracie and Crouch to join it at Al Abr in the Piper. The following story of its adventures is based on Ian Grimwood's careful report, which I have paraphrased with his kind permission.*

It took the convoy all day to do fifty miles up the steep escarpment to the plateau, where the first camp was made at 5500 feet above sea level. Next day the going was good and

*Grimwood, I. R., 'Operation Oryx', *Oryx Magazine*, vol. 6, 1962, pp. 308–34.

after seventy miles the deep Wadi Duan was reached. Driving on a rough track between cliffs 900 feet high, all went well until the first sand dunes were encountered. All the vehicles negotiated them successfully except the Ford catching car which, after a brief struggle and a screech of shattering metal from its gearbox, finally gave up the ghost. It was pushed to the nearby fort at Gaudah and abandoned. Next day the convoy reached Al Abr, having covered nearly 200 miles of atrocious tracks in three days. Here all the expedition members met together for the first time.

Late next day the expedition turned eastwards and headed across a sandy plain, planning to tackle the next lot of dunes in the cool of the following dawn. Camp was pitched on the edge of the dunes. The heavier vehicles did not arrive until ten o'clock at night and after refuelling and a hasty meal set off again so as to go as far as possible across the dunes before the sun rose. The lighter cars left around five and the Piper took off for its next landing, at Thamud.

The eastern route involved crossing the dunes at rightangles to their long ridges, each ascent being taken at top speed. Repeatedly the light vehicles were halted with spinning wheels, but the right technique was quickly learned and it was not long before the heavy convoy was passed. One truck had burnt out a main bearing. A radio message brought a truck from Thamud to pick up its load, while the Piper flew back to Mukalla for a new bearing. The organization was working well and when, after another seventy-five miles, the expedition reached Thamud, everyone enjoyed the welcoming party organized by the company commander at the little whitewashed fort. Its small garrison controlled the local blood feuds and tribal squabbles and guarded the only well in the region.

The final destination at Sanu was reached two days later. It was the last outpost of the Hadhrami Beduin Legion. On the way, the convoy had been twice halted by rifle fire from Beduin parties who merely asked politely for news of rain which their camels badly needed. The expedition was now in the area where the search for oryx could begin. A landing strip was made for the Piper and it was called in by radio. The only anxiety now was the loss of the specially built catching car. The adapted Bedford was less manoeuvrable and lacked the essential rapid acceleration.

After a day of preparation, the first hunting party set off at dawn. It consisted of four vehicles and was accompanied by an escort of ten soldiers and a sergeant who rendered magnificent service, particularly in overhauling the vehicles every night. The catching camp was set up and the aircraft with its native guide, Tomatum bin Harbi, was called in. Tomatum, in the absence of maps, played a vital part in the search for oryx; when later both the radio beacon and the ground radio failed, the Piper lost much of its value, but he turned out to be a superb tracker.

Next day only rhim gazelles were seen, but no oryx tracks. That evening, however, a Kathiri guard arrived at the camp with firm evidence that a few oryx had been seen forty miles to the north-east and fifty miles to the south-west. A search party was sent out and confirmed that tracks were found. Camp was moved to the nearer area, where noise and lights were kept to a minimum. At 4.30 next morning the catching team drove to the spot where the tracks had been found and a careful search was made over an area of twenty square miles.

It was a region of rolling dunes and gravel plains with rocky outcrops. In the depressions were tufts of sunburnt clump-grass. It looked as if no rain had fallen for several years, but in some of the deeper gullies the grass was still faintly green. This was the principal food of the oryx at this season and they would travel a hundred miles to find it. During that day four or five oryx tracks were sighted, but only one was less than ten days old. This was carefully followed and the uncanny skill of Tomatum and the Kathiri guard was fully demonstrated; on foot or even in a Land Rover travelling at nearly 20 mph they could follow a spoor invisible to Europeans.

After following the spoor for thirty-five miles the trackers reported it to be now only twelve hours old. Excitement began to rise. The oryx was heading northward purposefully towards a mile-wide wadi, where later wind-driven sand completely obliterated its tracks, which could not be re-located. Sadly the hunting party returned to camp. Round one to the oryx.

Before sunrise next morning the search began again and 125 miles were covered, every wadi being closely examined. The following day a really fresh track was found. While one car went ahead in a series of wide sweeps, the trackers followed the spoor relentlessly. Three hours later Grimwood caught sight through his binoculars of an oryx galloping over the crest of a dune and immediately gave chase, only to lose it in a series of stony wadis. It was round two to the oryx; but the patient trackers now found fresh droppings on the trail they were following and everyone concentrated on this prospect. An hour later, as they entered a small wadi, an oryx rose from under a bush and went off at full gallop, with the catcher car in close pursuit.

As the car closed the gap, the oryx made a half-hearted attempt to attack, swerving round across the front wheels. Too clumsy for close manoeuvre, the car struck it a glancing blow, rolling it over. It was unhurt and away immediately. Closing again, a noose was slipped over its head and the quarry was secured. It showed no fight and was quickly blindfolded, given an anti-shock injection and, after it had recovered its wind, was lifted carefully into the crate. Only eight minutes had elapsed since the animal had been sighted and it showed no sign of exhaustion. It was an adult male and surprisingly docile, making no protest when the ticks with which it was infested were removed from between its back legs. It was taken slowly back to Sanu, where it readily accepted food in its thatched holding pen. Round three had gone to the expedition and champagne was produced by the kindly Colonel Grey, Commander of the Hadhrami Beduin Legion. It is sad to relate that Colonel Grey, who had given such unstinted help to the expedition, was later ambushed and killed and his wife seriously wounded.

The search for oryx continued far and wide until 21 May,

by which time a female and two more males were successfully caught. Unfortunately one of the males had previously
been wounded by a .303 bullet and died soon after capture.
Nevertheless, though disappointed by the small number of
oryx caught or seen, the expedition had at least obtained the
bare nucleus of a breeding stock and it was time to prepare
for the 2000-mile journey back to Kenya.

At sunrise on 25 May a heavily laden RAF Beverley took
the expedition members to Aden, where they and the crated
oryx were transferred to a waiting Britannia and by mid-
afternoon were landed in Nairobi.

In London there was jubilation. Interest in the expedition
had been widespread and the London Zoo, which had the
only known oryx in captivity, moreover a female, had offered
to donate it to what was already being called 'the world
herd'. But if breeding was to succeed, the oryx would require
both highly skilled scientific management and the right
climatic conditions. The solution was found when the
Zoological Society of Arizona offered the facilities of its
admirable zoo at Phoenix. There the captive oryx could
have large, isolated enclosures and expert supervision, in a
climate approximating to that of the Aden Protectorate. The
Shikar-Safari Club of Los Angeles, who had already contributed generously to the cost of the expedition, offered to
pay for flying the animals from Kenya to the United States.
The offers were accepted gratefully and not long after the
herd had reached Phoenix the first oryx calf was born in
captivity.

News of the expedition's success had of course reached all
the Arab countries and it was then learned that several of
the rulers had small private collections of oryx. The ruler of
Kuwait had two females, which he offered to the Fauna
Preservation Society. Unfortunately one died, but the other
was successfully added to the world herd. HM King Saud of
Saudi Arabia had eight and graciously donated two pairs to
the herd. (Since then the Saudi Arabian herd has been
excellently rehoused at Riyadh and now represents a valuable
insurance against disaster overtaking those at Phoenix.)

Today the world herd is breeding well and as this book goes to press consists of eighty-two animals. Part of the herd will shortly be moved to the Shaumari reserve in the Azraq National Park in Jordan, which had been created as a result of my expedition of 1963. Others may go to the Jiddat al Harisis reserve in Oman. As a precaution, some of the oryx have been dispersed to other highly skilled zoos. In private collections there are also a few in Saudi Arabia and Abu Dhabi and a fine herd of thirty-five at HE Sheikh Qassim's ranch at Soleimy, Qatar. The number of surviving wild oryx is still not known, though in 1972 it was reported that motorized raiders had killed at least another three and captured four others in Oman. Most of the Arab rulers have now forbidden the motorized hunting of oryx and it is hoped that a few of these noble creatures may still be roaming the vast deserts of south-east Arabia. Even so, their numbers must now be too small to represent a viable breeding population. Without the imaginative efforts of the Fauna Preservation Society and the World Wildlife Fund, and the many governments, zoos, scientific societies and commercial organizations which contributed to Operation Oryx, this unique species would almost certainly not have survived.

Ian Grimwood was awarded the gold medal of the World Wildlife Fund for the success of this particularly arduous expedition. In 1977 he received the J. Paul Getty Prize for his outstanding contributions to conservation.

2

A SINGLE-HANDED VICTORY

NOT all those who have earned renown as conservationists
are highly trained specialists with a string of academic
qualifications. Some are rank amateurs, who have learned
the hard way. Certainly none had a harder apprenticeship
than Kunwar Arjan Singh ('Billy' to his friends). He is by
nature a stubborn rebel against bureaucracy and has what
he calls 'a natural perversity of character' which enables him
to overcome difficulties by often very unorthodox means. As
an ex-soldier of the Indian army, he also has more than
average courage. I have known him for some years and every
time we meet he seems to be involved in a new scrape with
officialdom. It is true that small-town bureaucrats in India,
as in most countries, can be infuriatingly obstructive or
obtuse, but to anyone of Billy's impetuous nature, obstruc-
tion is simply intolerable. Such a philosophy is unusual in
India and does not fit in easily with the patient acceptance
of authority which is typical of the national scene.

Billy had the good fortune to be brought up in one of the
richest areas of wildlife in India, at Balrampur, close to the
south-western frontier of Nepal. His father managed the
affairs of the Maharajkunar, who at that time was a minor.
Like his father, Billy became a crack shot at an early age,
shooting his first leopard at the age of twelve and a tiger at
fourteen. Both animals were abundant in those days and
nobody thought twice about hunting them. From boyhood
until he joined the army, big-game shooting was his passion

and he spent most of his time in the magnificent forests of the region, gradually accumulating an intimate knowledge of all forms of wildlife. He remained with the army until he was twenty-eight. Times were difficult in India during the post-war years and it was not easy to find employment. He finally turned to farming, buying a remote tract of land near the Nepalese border at Pallia.

Characteristically, he chose the area for its abundant wildlife rather than for its agricultural potentiality. Indeed he knew very little about farming, but wanted an open-air life. The land looked anything but promising, being rough savanna with extensive tracts of tamarisk and swamp, over which innumerable domestic buffaloes and cattle wandered unattended. He had been warned that dacoits terrorized the neighbouring villages and that malaria was endemic in the region. However, being young and enthusiastic, these trifles did not disturb him. He set about the task of clearing the ground and building his home with tremendous energy. The labourers he hired did not share his enthusiasm, however, and worked at snail's pace. Accustomed to having his orders obeyed, he drove them hard, standing in the blazing sun all day until he collapsed with sunstroke.

He soon learned that his arrival at Pallia was far from welcome, particularly with the *gaddis* (graziers), who strongly objected to his insistence that their cattle should not graze on his land. The first fields of wheat and corn that he sowed were immediately destroyed by trespassing cattle and goats.

Appeals to the *gaddis* having been ignored, he tried to apply the legally approved remedy of rounding up the offending cattle and taking them to a pound. This also failed – the cattle were too wild to be caught and those of his men who did catch any were either bribed by the *gaddis* to release them, or were beaten up. The local authorities to whom he appealed turned a blind eye.

Lesser men might have given in, or succumbed to the pervasive practice of bribery, which in India has been almost sanctified by tradition. Billy was made of sterner stuff. Action

B

within the law having failed, he took matters into his own hands. He was losing money heavily by the destruction of his crops and had no intention of quitting. The next time he saw cattle feeding on a particularly fine crop of rice, he ordered his men to round them up. They succeeded in catching only two bullocks, which, being half-wild, attacked them repeatedly. In desperation, Billy seized his small .22 rifle and put a pellet in the knee of each beast to slow them down and they were successfully tethered. He then returned them to their owner, who promptly took him to court and enlisted the local newspaper to publish a violent attack on him as an army vandal who had outraged Hindu sentiment by wounding animals which they regarded as sacred. Billy settled out of court by paying the market price for the bullocks, which he then sold at a profit. On reflection, he felt he had won the first round.

But the battle continued and the graziers took no steps to curb their cattle. Billy retaliated by catching isolated animals and tethering them where they were killed at night by roaming tigers, afterwards removing the tether so that they could be regarded as having died by natural predation. The graziers riposted with a trumped-up charge that he had been seen to shoot a trespassing horse on one of his fields. A warrant was issued for his arrest, but the case was dropped when he threatened to prosecute the supposed witness for fabricating the evidence. On another occasion he caught a man on his property who threatened him with an axe and took him to the police station. The police, who were very much in league with the local people, blandly told him that as no blood had flowed, he could not prosecute. In India there is no point in being right if one is powerless and Billy recognized that the scales of justice were heavily loaded against him.

Nevertheless, as time passed, the *gaddis* gradually came to realize that this tough soldier could not be intimidated. Their minds were in any case now much preoccupied with the exploits of the local dacoits, who were regularly pillaging their homes and murdering any who resisted them. The police were good enough to warn Billy that his house had been marked down for a raid by the dacoits, but fortunately the leader was ambushed and killed just before the planned attack.

Meanwhile, Billy's farm was beginning to improve and he was able to turn his attention to the wild animals which raided his crops. Wild pigs and wild elephants were the chief culprits and he realized that farming in a region noted for its wildlife had its penalties. He shot a number of pigs, many of them monsters weighing 300 pounds and carrying eight-inch tushes. He could not bring himself to shoot elephants because they were becoming scarce in India, so he kept them off the crops by erecting tin cans on strings, the noise of which frightened them. Tigers, too, were a problem, for they liked to lie up with their cubs in his sugar cane. These he drove off by riding his elephant around them and firing blank cartridges.

For fourteen years he kept up the struggle to earn a livelihood as a farmer, gradually overcoming the many problems and perfecting his techniques. But the wildlife had become increasingly scarce and the area no longer pleased him. Malaria, which decimated the local population and made the recruitment of labour a constant difficulty, was a factor in his final decision to try again in a more favourable locality, where he could see more wildlife.

The area he chose was on the far side of the plain below the Dudwa Range, in the Kheri district of the State of Uttar Pradesh. It was even more isolated than Pallia. It was also much more beautiful, with high sal forest, on the edge of which he built his new home overlooking the plain and the confluence of the Neora and Soheli rivers. Wildlife was exceptionally abundant. Tigers and leopards were plentiful. Stately barasingha (swamp deer), chital (spotted deer), hog-deer, nilgai, sambur and blackbuck roamed the area and there were crocodiles and Gangetic dolphins in the river. Both langur and rhesus monkeys swarmed in the trees. Snakes were initially a problem, for cobras and deadly kraits were constantly unearthed when the ploughs began turning the soil in the new fields. But there were few difficulties with trespass by graziers, or from malaria and much less risk from dacoits. Billy was enchanted with his surroundings. He decided to call his new home 'Tiger Haven', in memory of his brother who, as a famous Air Vice-Marshal, had been nicknamed 'Tiger'.

For the first few years Billy was fully occupied converting wilderness into a model farm. Once this was achieved, he had time to reflect on the wildlife of the region. Everywhere else in India it was becoming increasingly rare as the human population inexorably expanded. He hunted very seldom now but found increasing pleasure simply in watching animals. He put out salt-licks for the deer and constructed *machans* (tree hides) where he could enjoy seeing them and other creatures going about their business undisturbed. Frequently he slept in the forest in order to see the activity at dawn. He also built a little summer-house around the base of a huge jamun tree by the river, where turtles and crocodiles basked in the shallows and deer, leopards and sloth bears came to drink. An orphaned leopard cub which had been rescued from an animal trader in Calcutta was his particular household pet. 'Cheetla', as he called it, used to follow him on his walks in the forest and he built a tree-house for it which he named 'Leopard Haven'. Visitors to 'Tiger Haven' were astonished to find a full-grown leopard roaming around the house like a huge domestic cat. 'Cheetla' was eventually replaced by an orphaned tiger cub.

Billy Arjan Singh is a pessimist about the survival of wildlife in India. In his book *Tiger Haven** he writes: 'The way events are now shaping, and unless our values and material attitudes change, wildlife in India cannot last beyond a decade or so . . . it is merely a question of time.' However, he wrote this before the Indian government's great six-year scheme to save the tiger, which is described elsewhere in the book, began to bear fruit. He was depressed and incensed by the massive destruction of forests and the slaughter of wildlife which was going on around him. Nobody seemed to care

*Singh, Arjan, *Tiger Haven*, Macmillan, London, 1973.

and least of all the government officials at that time. Hunting, trapping and poisoning, both legal and illegal, had run riot. Land for wildlife was visibly shrinking as more and more was taken over by the Punjabis who had swarmed into the area after Partition. Gun licences were issued on an uncontrolled scale, ostensibly for crop protection, but in reality as a matter of political patronage. There was no law to control shooting outside the forest areas and guns were freely used by an ever-increasing number of poachers, who preyed on deer and other animals whose meat or skins could be profitably sold.

The careful system of selective forest exploitation of the long-lived native trees, which expert British foresters had introduced long before Partition, had been replaced by a frantic and wholesale exploitation of everything which could be sold. Native trees were being replaced by fast-growing foreign species such as eucalyptus, which brought quick profit but could not sustain wildlife. Wherever he looked, he could see the impending doom of India's once fabulously rich natural heritage. Like the great Jim Corbett before him, Billy became a hunter turned conservationist, converted by the beauty, the innocence and the vulnerability of the animals he had once shot. More and more he devoted his energies to saving the wildlife and forests of his region from destruction.

He already leased a large tract of forest behind 'Tiger Haven'. With some twenty other landowners he applied each year for a renewal, but usually found that professional shikaris had been given first option in order to provide sport for rich visiting Americans. Sometimes he improved his chances by applying under four or five different names. When this failed, he went out at night and released the tethered buffaloes which the shikaris had put out to attract tigers. When he learned that visiting Americans were using lights for hunting at night and had shot a cub (both illegal practices) he reported them to the authorities, but, as usual, no action was taken.

One of his chief concerns at that time was to preserve the

beautiful barasingha deer. These fine animals had been
wiped out in most parts of India, the Ghola swamps some
eight miles from 'Tiger Haven' being one of their last
refuges. In 1964, when the State Wildlife Board was created,
Billy became one of its members. He strongly recommended
that the 3000 acres of the Ghola swamps should be given
protection in perpetuity. Dr George Schaller, the famous
American wildlife scientist, examined the area with Billy and
found that the population of barasingha had already dropped
from the previous level of 1500 to only 600. This was, however, still the largest surviving group in India. The State
Wildlife Board took two years to make up its mind to accept
Billy's recommendation, but by then it was too late, an
extremist political group known as the Naxalites having
illegally taken possession of the swamps. The barasingha were
quickly scattered by gun and plough. Infuriated, Billy
watched the deer dispersing over the countryside, where
hunters awaited them. Some, however, entered the 'Tiger
Haven' area and this gave him an idea. He would try to
drive them into this sanctuary.

Barasingha do not live in the harsh, sun-baked plains, but
in moist deciduous forests; therefore the first thing was to
provide plenty of grazing for them in the forest glades. With
typical energy, he ploughed up a number of five-acre plots
in the reserved forest and sowed them with grass, well knowing that the authorities would strenuously disapprove. There
would be time to argue about that later; meanwhile not a
minute was to be lost. Around the plots he made salt-licks,
which he knew the deer greatly liked. The grass had scarcely
emerged before he was challenged by the forestry department, who accused him of ploughing up government land.
Almost miraculously, he succeeded in convincing them that
what he had done did not harm the forest.

The next inevitable problem was with graziers, whose
cattle quickly found the succulent new grass. Appeals to
them having, as usual, no effect, Billy once again resorted to
strong-arm methods. The next grazier to appear with his
cattle was seized and tethered to the towing-hook of Billy's

jeep and at walking pace towed protesting out of the forest. This action resulted in another prosecution, but as no bodily harm could be proved by the grazier, the case was dismissed. However, the graziers gave the area a wide berth thereafter.

The next task was to move the barasingha remaining in the Ghola swamps into the new grazing area. This was accomplished with the aid of six elephants, which were slowly ridden in line abreast, to the accompaniment of much shouting and the firing of blank cartridges. Some 250 deer were successfully shepherded into the forest, where they soon settled.

The local poachers, who had watched the proceedings, soon began shooting the deer, obliging Billy to patrol the forest at frequent intervals by day and night until he was physically exhausted. He appealed to the State Wildlife Board to declare the area a protected reserve and to exclude all graziers. This was strongly opposed by a local politician, who needed the votes of the graziers and also by the professional shikaris, who automatically opposed anything likely to reduce their sport or opportunities to make money. Once again Billy was facing a united opposition, but he fought on, grimly determined to save the steadily declining herd of barasingha. A whole year passed in fruitless argument and then a ray of light appeared. A new State Minister of Forests recognized the importance of saving wildlife. To Billy's delight and astonishment, the Minister decided that 82·2 square miles surrounding 'Tiger Haven' should become a wildlife reserve; this included a 25-mile frontage below the estate and a belt of forest three miles deep behind it, towards the Nepalese frontier. Thus the barasingha, the local tigers and many other much persecuted animals would have a real chance of survival. Today, some ten years after the reserve was created, the number of barasingha has risen from the original 250 to about 1250 animals.

I should perhaps at this point interject a few words about the two races of the barasingha. The northern race, with which Arjan Singh was dealing at Dudwa, now occurs only in northern India, in the states of Uttar Pradesh and Assam and in south-western Nepal. Its total surviving population, including a few stragglers in Bhutan, is in the region of 3000. The southern race, which differs in having narrower hooves more suited to the harder ground it occupies, has been very nearly exterminated by the exploitation of its traditional grazing areas for forestry or agriculture. The only remaining population is in the Kanha National Park in the State of Madhya Pradesh. Both races have now been closely studied under research projects financed by the World Wildlife Fund. Conservation programmes have been introduced for the northern race at the Sukla Phanta Reserve in Nepal and the Kaziranga National Park in Assam and for the southern at Kanha. Both races require swampy grasslands, with plentiful access to water during the dry season, but the southern needs a drier, rather less swampy habitat, of sal forest with grassy glades. The saving of the southern population at Kanha was another fine success story, thanks chiefly to the work of a Swiss scientist, Claude Martin, and M. S. Panwar, the Director of the reserve. By careful management of the grazing areas and water sources and by excluding poachers, domestic cattle and forestry operations, a remarkable recovery was effected. The southern barasingha population in 1969 was only 66; by 1977 it has risen to nearly 250. The area of the Kanha National Park has since been increased from 122 square miles to 363, as part of the conservation initiative arising from 'Operation Tiger' (see Chapter 12).

One would have thought that after such a triumphant success, Billy Arjan Singh would have been content to settle down to enjoy life. He is not that kind of man, however. He wanted to improve the reserve and was soon involved once again in overcoming difficulties with the Forestry Department, with poachers, with graziers, with honey-collectors, with hunters and with the aboriginal Tharu tribesmen who inhabited the forest along the Nepalese border. As soon as these troubles had been more or less controlled, he turned his attention to the wildlife of the river and particularly to saving the mugger, or marsh crocodile, and its even rarer relative the narrow-snouted fish-eating gharial, both of which were being steadily exterminated by skin-traders. In this, too, he was finally successful, obtaining official sanction to exclude all crocodile-hunters for two miles along the river on either side beyond the boundaries of his property. This secured sufficiently long stretches of muddy or sandy river banks for the crocodiles to lay their eggs and perpetuate their kind.

Billy did all this single-handed. He now rarely carried a gun except when a man-eating tiger had been identified. In such cases he insisted on dispatching it himself rather than allow the trigger-happy professionals or forest guards to shoot the wrong animal by mistake. Instead of a gun, he usually carried a camera, or ciné equipment. The standard of the pictures he obtained was remarkably high, though he was entirely self-taught.

In March 1972 the World Wildlife Fund asked the well-known French wildlife photographer Christian Zuber to visit Dudwar and take pictures of Billy Arjan Singh's reserve. Chris Zuber has made many magnificent films about animals in several continents and he does great work for conservation through his television series in France and elsewhere. He was delighted by the prospect of filming tigers, but arrived at 'Tiger Haven' at a time when Billy was having sleepless nights because of a fresh outbreak of poaching. A number of tigers had been killed or wounded in or around the reserve.

On the last night of Chris's visit, his pretty young wife, Nadine, and the local wildlife officer decided to take a short drive in the forest to see nocturnal animals in the headlights. Five miles from the house they came across a large tigress lying exhausted by the road with one of its fore-paws caught in a heavy steel trap set by poachers. Chris was quickly on the scene to take flashlight pictures of the poor beast, which were later used all over the world in support of the WWF tiger campaign. While he was engaged in this task, there was a sudden alarm as the headlights of the jeep illuminated the eyes of another tiger approaching. The driver, in his fright, put his fist on the horn and gunned the engine. The tiger withdrew into the darkness. Chris ignored it. His concern was for the poor tigress, which was thrashing around and tugging at its mutilated paw in the jaws of the trap. He wanted to send for a tranquillizing dart-gun, so that the animal could be examined and released, but realized that as it was nearly midnight, this would not be possible until dawn.

Billy, Chris and Nadine returned to the spot at daybreak, only to find that the tigress had torn its foot out of the trap, leaving a trail of blood-spots as she retreated towards the river. The poachers had already sneaked back to retrieve the trap. Riding elephants, the little party set out on the dangerous mission of trying to locate the injured and doubtless very angry tigress. Billy had his rifle; Chris and Nadine were armed only with cameras, but insisted on accompanying him. They failed to locate it, though a dozen more traps were found carefully camouflaged. Happily, because he knew the stripe-patterns of all the local tigers, Billy was able to identify the tigress after the Zubers had left. It had apparently recovered.

The only thing about which Billy remained dissatisfied now was the size of the reserve. He thought longingly of the thousands of square miles of unspoilt country embraced by some of the great African and American national parks. Dudwa's eighty-two square miles was a flea-bite by comparison. It must be enlarged! With his usual determination he threw himself into the new task, bombarding the authorities with plans and recommendations.

Local politicians, with an eye on votes, and the bureaucrats with their usual sycophantic determination to win favour with the politicians, murmured about the need for more land for the peasant-farmers. Billy knew that more land for the peasants did not necessarily mean the production of more food, but it *did* mean increasing the number of starving cattle to roam the plain and the forest. As he says in his book: 'Most of India's 300 million cattle do not give an ounce of milk and religious sentiments prevent them from being slaughtered either for food or leather.' What was the point of giving more land for unproductive farming, when this only meant more ravenous cattle to turn farming land into desert? It was a political gesture completely out of touch with reality. The real need was to teach the farmers to make more productive use of the land, to supply them with cheaper fertilizers and better equipment. Above all to recognize the intolerable burden which reverence for the cow imposed on India's hungry millions.

The World Wildlife Fund was keenly interested in Billy's one-man crusade on behalf of the wildlife of Dudwa and had given him a new jeep and a small tractor for patrolling and improving the reserve. A number of well-known conservationists had also admired his work. The then Prime Minister, Indira Gandhi, herself an ardent conservationist, was increasingly sympathetic in smoothing over some of the political obstacles to his plans. Although he had never endeared himself to the authorities, his achievements were undeniable and too obvious to be ignored much longer.

Finally the state government of Uttar Pradesh took the momentous decision to create a new national park, with the Dudwa reserve as its inner sanctuary. The whole region was put under official protection and was gazetted in the summer of 1976. Billy's ten-year battle was over. His success in saving the barasingha and tigers and their forest habitat at Dudwa had qualified the reserve for inclusion in the new national conservation plan.

Dudwa National Park is a permanent monument to one man's single-minded effort. The fact that he had no scientific training yet never put a foot wrong in the ecological planning of the reserve, makes his achievement all the more remarkable. If he won some of his battles by unorthodox and sometimes pretty rough tactics, one can only say that he was a fighting crusader and that the end justified the means. When at the end of 1976 he received the gold medal of the World Wildlife Fund in San Francisco, the loudest of the applause came from the professional conservationists of many nations who were present. Billy, the hunter turned conservationist, had won their whole-hearted respect.

3

THE GOLDEN FLEECE

In the bitterly cold atmosphere of a grassy plateau 16000 feet above sea level, the air was noticeably rarefied. The fitful sunlight to the east revealed the stupendous snowy peaks of the Peruvian Andes stretching like a gigantic wall as far as the eye could reach. Westward towards Lima were lesser mountains, descending to cultivated hills as they neared the far distant Pacific Ocean, which lay hidden beneath its invariable blanket of coastal clouds. Deep gorges isolated the plateau from all but skilled mountaineers. The temperature was too low for the sun to melt the frozen lip of the distant snowfields and thus provide water for the brown and parched vegetation in the valleys far below, but the short grass on the plateau was kept green all the year round by rain, or by the low clouds which periodically blotted out the region. This was the *puna* zone of the Cordilleras.

The only sign of life was a scattered group of tawny-coated, rather gazelle-like animals with tufts of fleecy white hair drooping from their long necks. They were small, barely thirty inches at the shoulder, and they were cropping the grass hungrily. From time to time the single male among them lifted his head to make sure no danger threatened his harem in this landscape of icy desolation. Spaced at regular intervals across the plateau were strangely symmetrical black mounds of dung, to which the animals trotted occasionally, to add their quotas in a ritual blindly followed by their kind for generation after generation. They were vicuñas, survivors of a species which had once been numerous in the highlands from Ecuador through Peru and Bolivia to Chile and north-western Argentina.

The vicuña is the smallest and rarest of the four cameloid animals which occur in Latin America. Their common ancestor is thought to have lived in the western part of North America during the Eocene period; in the following millions of years its descendants wandered across the world and evolved into the two camels and four cameloids which we know today. Only two of the latter, the vicuña and the guanaco, are true wild species. The llama is the best-known of the South American group. It originated from the wild guanaco and has been the principal beast of burden since the days of the Incas. It also plays a primary role in the economy of the Andean Indians, who use its long, shaggy wool for clothing and rope-making, its flesh for food, its milk for drinking, its fat for candles and its dung for fuel. In the bitterly cold nights of the *puna* zone the Indians, like their Inca forebears, huddle against their llamas for warmth while sleeping. According to the detailed records of the *conquistadores*, llamas suffered from endemic syphilis which they passed on to the Incas, who in turn infected their Spanish overlords and thus transmitted the disease to Europe. In fact, the disease was common in Europe before the Spanish conquest of Peru, having been brought back to Spain in 1493 by the followers of Christopher Columbus. Because of the llamas' value to them, the Indians treat them with care, though they are bad-tempered beasts, prone to kick unpredictably and to spit regurgitated cud. One which I incautiously photographed at Machu Picchu, the lost cloud-city of the pre-Incas, spat with devastating accuracy into the lens of my camera.

The alpaca, smaller, more bulky and more variegated in colour than the llama, has also been a domestic animal since the twelfth century. Like the llama, its wild ancestor was the guanaco. The domestic flocks are usually kept at above the 12 000 foot level and are sheared every two years. To improve the quality of its wool, the alpaca has been crossed with both the llama and the vicuña, but such hybrids tend to be sterile.

The fourth member is the guanaco, which more closely resembles the vicuña in its slender form, though it is a larger animal. It is a shy and very alert creature which has become increasingly rare. Unlike the vicuña, however, it has a rather coarse brown coat of little commercial value. Its range extends from about 13000 feet down to the semi-desert coastal plains; it occurs also in the lowlands in Paraguay, Argentina and Patagonia. Both these wild species have long canine teeth with which they can inflict severe wounds in defence of their young. Of the four, I find the ungainly llama, with its uncertain temper and disagreeable expression, the least attractive. The shy and dainty vicuña, on the other hand, with its silky white jabot, Disneyesque baby face and soulful eyes beneath ridiculously long, film-star eyelashes, is irresistible. Its incomparably soft wool has been woven and worn by man since 5000 BC. Like the beautiful little chinchilla, which shares the Andean heights with it, this has been its undoing. The remarkable light weight of the fur of both species is an evolutionary adaptation of importance to survival, for at such altitudes neither animal nor man can climb or move about quickly if impeded by a heavy coat.

The Incas had believed the vicuña to be the daughter of Pachamama, the goddess of fertility, and therefore sacred. Only the privileged Virgins of the Sun were permitted to weave its feather-light fleece and only royalty could wear it. For a commoner to kill a vicuña meant death after torture which the Incas had developed to a fine art. But apart from these religious scruples, the Incas had very advanced ideas about what we now call conservation. Their respect for wildlife extended to an obvious understanding of the value of wise land-use policies, from which developed their famous anti-erosion terracing and extensive irrigation schemes, examples of which can be seen to this day. Unlike their destructive present-day descendants, the Incas recognized the scarcity of forests in the high Andes and protected every wooded valley by law. They firmly believed that fur-bearing animals should be cropped selectively, on what we now term a sustained-yield basis, so that breeding stocks were never endangered.

A very full eye-witness account of the Inca's attitude towards the vicuña is contained in *The Royal Commentaries* written by Garcilesco de la Vega (1529–1616). He was himself the son of an Inca princess and a *conquistador*. According to his book, hunting was organized on strictly controlled lines. When the Lord-Inca decreed that a *chaco*, or royal hunt, should take place, tens of thousands of beaters surrounded the chosen area and in the course of a week or more all the animals were driven slowly to the centre, where the deer and other species required for food were speared or clubbed and their meat dried and distributed. Vicuña, however, were never killed, but captured with nets; after being carefully shorn of their wool, they were released unharmed. In order that wildlife should maintain its numbers by undisturbed breeding and to give vicuñas time to grow fresh wool, hunting sites were rotated on a four-year basis. Had the Incas themselves not been exterminated completely by the *conquistadores* in the eighteenth century, we would probably not only now be learning how best to look after wildlife.

The arrival of the Spanish and Portuguese in Central and South America heralded a determined slaughter not only of the native populations in the name of Christianity, but also of fur-bearing animals for personal gain or adornment. It did not take the Spanish long to discover the unique properties of the vicuña's wool and they were killed at a rate of 80000 a year until the survivors retreated into the safety of the inaccessible highlands of the Andes. By the time Simon Bolivar liberated Peru, there were none left in the foothills. In 1825 he published a decree protecting vicuñas and offering a large prize to anyone who succeeded in domesticating the species. So important did he consider the animal to be that he introduced it into the coat of arms of Peru. Successive artists changed it, however, into the more familiar llama which the coat of arms now bears.

For the following hundred years the vicuñas were left in relative peace, while the gun-toting South Americans indulged in a series of revolutions and wars which kept them too busy to find time for hunting at high altitudes.

A new chapter opened during the flamboyant Prohibition era in the United States, when leading gangsters and male film-stars took to wearing flashy thousand-dollar topcoats made from vicuña wool. The fashion quickly spread to Europe. The delighted fur traders bombarded their Latin American agents with orders for the precious fleeces which could earn such riches. Prices soared and the organized hunting of vicuñas began in earnest.

As the numbers of vicuñas in Peru, Bolivia, Chile and Argentina declined, so the efforts of the hunters increased. The trouble was that when a vicuña was killed it yielded only 150 grammes (less than half a pound) of ultra-lightweight wool. To weave one of the highly prized *colcha* blankets therefore required the killing of about 250 vicuñas. One Bolivian exporter alone was responsible for the death of 30000 in a single year, all the wool from which was exported to the United States. An even more deadly but more lucrative trade developed by the sale of so-called 'vicuñita' robes, made from the skins of new-born vicuña lambs, which, being easy to catch even by unarmed Indians, were killed in thousands. Unfortunately the reproductive rate of the species is very low, only a single lamb being produced at birth and these suffer a high natural mortality from the severe climate, foxes and pampas cats. Condor vultures, which are attracted by the placentas of new-born lambs, are said to drive lambs over precipices in order to kill them. When Peru finally banned the export of vicuña wool, smuggling became big business, the fleeces being hidden inside bales of wool from domestic sheep or alpacas, which were easily taken through customs and thence to Bolivia for shipment to Europe or America. The dimensions of the financial inducement to smugglers can be judged from the fact that by 1976 the woven fabric of illegally obtained vicuña wool had reached the astonishing figure of £450 per square metre. It was indeed a golden fleece.

Apart from professional hunters, the native Indians of the

The Arabian oryx was saved from extinction by capturing the last survivors, breeding them in captivity and restoring the offspring to protected reserves.

An oryx killed by motorized Arab hunters. This handsome species, which was once common throughout the Arabian deserts, has been mercilessly persecuted.

The very high prices paid for the 'golden fleece' of the vicuña
threatened the species with extinction throughout its entire
range in the Andes. The creation of reserves in Peru, Bolivia,
Chile and Argentina now ensures their future.

Opposite above: The two races of the Barasingha swamp deer
survive only in a few protected reserves in India and Nepal, where
they are now increasing.

Opposite below: Billy Arjan Singh with a young pet tiger. The
Dudwa National Park was created by his personal crusade to
save the Barasingha swamp deer and the tiger.

A sick baby orang-utan rescued from an animal dealer. The mothers are shot in order to obtain the babies, few of which survive for long in captivity.

Andes had also taken a toll of vicuñas, though their weapons were mostly old-fashioned muzzle loaders and the killing chiefly for meat. In recent years, however, a more serious additional threat developed when mineral prospectors working for North American companies took to hunting vicuñas as a pastime. They were soon joined by their city friends and by the local police who, under the guise of protecting the hunting parties, openly took part in the sport even in areas where the animals were legally protected. It seemed that the vicuña, like so many other defenceless and harmless creatures, was doomed everywhere. Between 1950 and 1970 at least 400000 had been killed. By then Peru, the main stronghold of the species, had only 9000 left. Bolivia had fewer than 1000, Chile only 700, while in Argentina the vicuña was already regarded as probably extinct.

In the late 1950s, however, there had emerged a Peruvian who really cared about the vicuña and was determined to save it. His name was Felipe Benavides. His background gave no hint that he was later to become one of the best-known conservationists in South America, though as a boy he had been fond of the colourful parrots and other wildlife in his father's garden. His father had been the Peruvian ambassador in London and he himself naturally followed a diplomatic career, serving with distinction in London, Stockholm and New York, where he was Consul General. When in 1954 he retired to Lima he began to take a serious interest in his country's wildlife. What he discovered shocked him profoundly. Peru had a bad name abroad for the exploitation of wildlife and everyone seemed to be engaged either in hunting or in destroying forests, or in making money by the sale of skins or live animals. Looking up the official records, he learned that nearly 140000 Peruvian monkeys of various kinds had been exported in five years and that for every animal which reached the port of departure alive, four or five more had died *en route*. About 1000 jaguar skins and 10000 ocelot skins left Peru every year. A single merchant had exported 36650 skins of South American sealions and fur seals in four months. Both Peruvian and foreign whaling ships, having killed off most of the sperm whales, were killing an increasing number of fin whales, blue whales and humpback whales in Peruvian waters. And so the records of slaughter went on. Determined to see for himself, Benavides visited the Andes, to look for vicuñas. He could not locate a single one. 'It was horrible!' he recalled. 'There was not a single conservationist in the country. I *had* to do something about it.'

Felipe Benavides has an impressive personality. Tall, handsome, always impeccably dressed, and multi-lingual, he commands attention wherever he goes. Though he looks like the traditional urbane stage diplomat, his voluble denunciation of the exploiters of wildlife often has little of the suavity of diplomacy and can be explosive and ruthless. He began his crusade by bombarding the press and magazines of Latin America with protests and denunciations, with particular reference to the vicuña. Then, realizing that the key to the suppression of the export of wildlife products lay with the foreign buyers, he extended his campaign to the United States and Europe. At every important international meeting concerned with conservation, he was there to protest about the exploitation of South American wildlife. Whether the occasion was appropriate or not, one could be sure that sooner or later the elegant figure of Benavides would rise and that, with eyes flashing, he would denounce at least one government for failure to pay attention to his exhortations. Ambassadors and government officials in country after country were approached and if necessary bullied into co-operation. On visits to Paris and London he did not hesitate to tell press conferences what he thought about local fashion houses which sold vicuña garments or the furs of jaguars and ocelots. Because reporters love a dramatic speaker, he got a good coverage. For a professional diplomat he could on occasion be astonishingly indiscreet, as, for example, when he publicly rebuked Prime Minister Fidel Castro of Cuba for accepting the gift of a vicuña poncho from the Chilean government.

On each Independence Day in Peru Benavides renews in

the press his attack on the government for its failure to reinstate the vicuña on the national coat of arms. He may yet succeed. Meanwhile he has the satisfaction of having succeeded in 1962 in having the vicuña engraved on Peru's coinage.

When the World Wildlife Fund was created in 1961, Benavides quickly buttonholed the President, HRH Prince Bernhard, urging him to make representations to the governments of Peru and Bolivia concerning the vicuña. Experts from the International Union for Conservation of Nature, who act as scientific advisers to the WWF, were brought in to examine the subject. Here at last Benavides could talk to the world's leading conservationists, who could analyse the problems in depth and who knew the right way to set about overcoming them. Exhortation was one thing, but if an endangered animal species was to be saved, it was first necessary to know exactly how it lived, what its ecological requirements were and above all to learn its exact status and distribution. It was decided that several experts should be sent to South America to conduct these studies. Meanwhile, steps would be taken to obtain the active co-operation of the various governments concerned.

The first breakthrough came in 1963, when the Peruvian government appointed the Servicio Forestal y de Casa to assume responsibility for the protection of wildlife. Two years later came the creation of a National Vicuña Reserve of 124000 acres in the Pampas Galeras region of Lucanas Province, in the Peruvian Andes. This area had just been examined in detail by P. V. Pierret, a wildlife expert from FAO, who had reported that it contained about 1000 vicuñas. The reserve was not created without considerable difficulty, two guards and a guide being killed by vicuña poachers in the process. Meanwhile, Ian Grimwood had been sent by the World Wildlife Fund to make a two-year study of the status of South American wildlife, which of course included the vicuña. Having roughed it in the wilds for many years, Grimwood was fully capable of exploring the difficult and sometimes dangerous jungles of the Amazon basin,

where many of the rarer animals lived, and, having been
Chief Game Warden in Kenya, he was accustomed to dealing
with armed poachers. His painstaking work later led to the
establishment of some of the most important wildlife reserves
in South America.

At about this time Felipe Benavides achieved another
breakthrough in the signing of what came to be called the
La Paz Agreement, by which Peru and its neighbouring
states formally decided to ban the traffic in vicuña wool.
However, though the agreement was important, there was a
long way to go before the now highly organized smuggling
racket, which involved the widespread bribery of officials,
could be brought under control. Effective supervision of
thousands of miles of frontiers was an almost insuperable task.
Obviously the only way of halting the continuing decline of
the vicuña was to strangle the apparently inexhaustible
demand at its source in the United States and Europe. In
1970 Great Britain and the United States banned the impor-
tation of vicuña products and a major step forward came
when the Convention on International Trade in Endangered
Species of Wild Fauna and Flora came into force in 1975.
By 1977 forty-one nations were parties to this Convention,
which imposed strict controls on the export or import of
species or their products listed in three appendices. The
vicuña was placed in Appendix 1, which amounted to a total
ban on trade. Conservationists now had an instrument of
real power and the hitherto almost unchecked losses of
endangered wildlife by commercial exploitation were controlled. Not only Peru, but Bolivia, Chile and Argentina had
by then given legal protection to the vicuña and all were
now planning to establish special reserves for it. Losses by
poaching were continuing, though on a reduced scale.
Unscrupulous dealers had already adopted various devices to
circumvent the new laws, such as describing vicuña wool as
'alpaca' in customs declarations, but their days were
numbered.

There remained the problem of restoring the now very
small population of vicuñas, which were scattered over a

huge area of the Andes. Thanks to the explorations of Ian Grimwood, Carl Koford, Hartmut Jungius and Jeffery Boswall, these were gradually located in all four countries, most of the explorations being financed by the World Wildlife Fund and the Frankfurt Zoological Society, though Jeffery Boswall made his discoveries in Argentina while filming wildlife for the BBC. National parks or reserves were established in Chile through the initiative of Mr J. Rottmann and the Corporación Forestal, in Bolivia through the Wildlife Service and in particular by Dr A. Cardozo, Ing. P. Baptista and G. Bejarano. In Peru by the Forest Service under the driving leadership of Dr M. Dourojeanni and Ing. C. Ponce. By 1977 the status of the vicuña had been revolutionized and the population had risen to an estimated total of nearly 50 000. Of these, there were at least 35 000 in or around the Pampas Galeras Reserve in Peru and nearly 2000 in Bolivia, many of which were in the Ulla-Ulla Reserve spanning the frontier between Bolivia and Peru and in the Bolivian Huancaroma Reserve. In the Lauca National Park in Chile there were about 1000 and in the newly created San Guillermo Reserve in Argentina around 8000. The vicuña was no longer an endangered species.

Scientists in the Pampas Galeras are now studying means by which some of the animals in the reserves might be periodically rounded up and sheared, in the manner so successfully practised by the Incas. The wool would, of course, be handled under special licence and the funds raised used to offset the cost of guarding and maintaining the reserves. If they succeed in emulating the methods of the Incas, the history of the vicuña will have turned full circle.

In 1973 Prince Bernhard bestowed the Order of the Golden Ark on Felipe Benavides 'for energetic leadership in wildlife conservation in Latin America and in particular for his part in saving the vicuña'. In 1975 he was awarded the J. Paul Getty Conservation Prize in recognition of the success of his crusade. The award, which is worth $50 000, has been described in the press as 'a kind of Nobel Prize for conservation'. It was typical of Felipe that he should immediately decide to devote it to the creation of a wildlife research station and a national park of 365000 hectares at Paracas, extending for forty miles along Peru's coast. This was gazetted in November 1976. Now President of Pro Defensa de la Naturaleza (the World Wildlife Fund organization in Peru), he maintains that his crusade is by no means over yet. His next objective is to re-introduce surplus vicuñas from Peru into the highlands of Ecuador, which the species once occupied.

4

THE RED APE PIONEERS

EVERY time I visit South-East Asia I come away reluctantly, longing to spend more time in its mysterious forests and among its friendly and industrious people. Its richness in wildlife of all kinds is almost incredible. It has, for example, 25000 flowering plants, compared with Europe's 3000. Borneo alone has more than 2200 different species of trees, compared with ten to twelve in the average European forest. In Malaya Alfred Russel Wallace was able to find 2000 different kinds of beetles in a single square mile of forest. As for mammals and birds, great and small, the region has a positively bewildering variety. Only naturalists who have lived there can have any real comprehension of the diversity of life which pullulates in the vast rain-forests and rivers.

Two such people are Barbara Harrisson and Dr John MacKinnon who, like Wallace a hundred years before them, fell completely under the spell of the islands of Borneo and Sumatra.

The old Borneo, as such, of course no longer exists as a political entity. After the British and Dutch withdrew from the East Indies, the north part of the huge island consisting of the states of Sarawak and Sabah became part of Malaysia, with the tiny British Protectorate of Brunei sandwiched between them. The remainder, now called Kalimantan went, like the rest of the immense archipelago stretching eastward towards New Guinea, to the new nation of Indonesia.

Barbara Harrisson and John MacKinnon had one other

thing in common – an absorbing interest in that most engaging of Asian animals, the orang-utan. Both made major contributions to our knowledge of this little-known species, which hitherto had been surrounded by a confusing web of anecdotal misinformation. Barbara's work was chiefly concerned with the rescue and rearing of captive baby orangs, in which she found herself involved at first only by mere chance. John was an experienced young scientist, who was determined to do what nobody had previously attempted, to study orangs by literally living among them for months at a time in their native rain-forest. Though others have done valuable work on this animal, these two were, in my opinion, the pioneers. Between them they did for the orang-utan what Jane Goodall and Hugo van Lawick did for the chimpanzee and George Schaller for the gorilla. All of them produced films and beautifully illustrated books, which have made the lives and problems of their subjects known to millions.

Barbara Harrisson and her husband Tom had a charming house at Kuching, the romantic old capital of Sarawak. It was the kind of untidily characterful home, crammed with books and old Bornean treasures, around which Somerset Maugham could have woven an immortal story. The kind of place which, to quote Barbara, was so overflowing that there was never room to put anything away. Dr Tom Harrisson was Director of the Sarawak Museum and knew more about the island, its people and its wildlife than anyone since the days of Rajah Brooke. He was a scientist, with deep convictions about the hard realities of conservation, viewing his wife's enthusiastic efforts on behalf of the orang-utan with a kind of amused tolerance. Nevertheless he contributed to her charmingly illustrated book about them and was probably as surprised as she was when it received wide acclaim in the scientific as well as the popular press.*

To appreciate the pioneering nature of Barbara's work, one had only to examine the scanty background to man's

*Harrisson, Barbara, *Orang-utan*, Collins, London, 1962.

interest in the orang-utan and the almost complete failure of the world's zoos to understand the requirements of the species in captivity.

As far back as 35 000 BC prehistoric man is known from archaeological remains to have eaten orangs in localities as far apart as China and the island of Celebes (now called Sulawesi). Today the distribution of the species has been reduced to only two countries. Indonesia has remnant populations in southern and north-eastern Kalimantan and at the northern end of Sumatra. Malaysia has some in western Sarawak and eastern Sabah. European civilization had no knowledge of the animal until the seventeenth century, when the first of many highly dramatized and wildly inaccurate stories of a terrifying sub-human creature inhabiting what was then called the Malay Archipelago began to circulate. It was said to stand six feet tall, to have herculean strength, to throw rocks, to be able to speak and to abduct or rape women at will.

The first English traveller actually to see orang-utans in the wild was Captain Daniel Beeckman, who in 1714 published an account of them in his book *A Voyage to and from Borneo*. He called them 'oran-ootans', but strangely described them as hairless, whereas they are noticeably hairy creatures. Until very recent times zoology depended very largely on the examination of bones or carcasses rather than knowledge of live animals. Even the great Wallace, who spent two years in Borneo in the 1850s, made most of his observations from specimens which he shot. The scarcity of orang-utans in museums led to much argument about the selection of a correct scientific name for the species. Linnaeus had classified it as a hominid, with the name *Homo sylvestris orang-utang*, whereas today we call it *Pongo pygmaeus*, a name which to my mind does less than justice to so fine and large an animal. The Malay name, correctly spelt *orang-utan*, literally 'man of the jungle', has been almost universally adopted for common use, though in Sarawak the Dyak people call it *maias* and the Dusuns of Sabah *mawas*.

The human exploitation of orang-utans is as disgraceful a

story as any to be found. Bearing in mind that it concerns a very advanced primate, probably as capable of suffering as any human being, it also involved an excessive degree of cruelty. From the nineteenth century onwards private individuals and animal traders made countless attempts to capture orang-utans and transport them to Europe or America; but it was not until 1926 that an adult from Sumatra, purchased for £4000, managed to survive in the Dresden zoo for two years. All the others died within a few weeks. Collectors then turned their attention to catching baby orangs, a practice which is still continuing. This involved shooting the mothers while they are carrying young. A few of the babies may survive her fall from the tree, but three or four females may be shot for every baby secured alive. The subsequent mortality of the infants in unskilled hands is appalling and very few reach their intended destinations alive. Many are sold to private individuals in Indonesia, where until very recently the ownership of a pet orang-utan was regarded as a status symbol. Even today in the leading zoos of the world, which are directed by capable scientists, orang-utans do not thrive. Usually they become very fat, lethargic and die prematurely. Their breeding record in captivity has until very recent years been abysmal.

Whereas the two other world-famous apes, the gorilla and the chimpanzee, are highly territorial animals, living in a complex social order, the orang-utan is a solitary creature and a constant maverick, moving alone or in small family groups from one fruiting tree to another and occupying a tree-top nest or sleeping platform only so long as is necessary to strip the tree of its fruit before moving on. It is shy and elusive. Living in almost impenetrable rain-forests, it is exceptionally difficult to study in the wild. In spite of the fanciful stories of it attacking humans and tearing off their limbs or raping women, it is normally gentle and self-effacing, preferring to slip away unseen at the approach of humans. All it demands of life is ample food, the affection of its kind and leisure for fun – for in the wild orangs indulge in constant play even when alone.

In colouration orangs are usually reddish-orange. Their fur is wispy and upstanding, so that when the sun is behind them they appear to move within an orange halo. In old age their colour darkens to purplish-brown or even black. The adults are handsomely bearded, though the upper lip remains hairless and grey. Old males grow so large and heavy that they can no longer swing with supple grace through the tree-tops, but have to spend much of their time foraging on the ground, where, doubtless feeling more vulnerable, they sometimes act aggressively if surprised by man. The prominent fleshy pouches which older males grow around their faces give them a rather terrifying appearance. When wounded or cornered they will of course bite severely and are certainly powerful enough to kill a man, but stories of their actually doing so are largely apocryphal.

Baby orangs are just about the most human and appealing little mites it is possible to imagine and their behaviour would melt the hardest heart. Barbara Harrisson is a naturally warm-hearted person. When, therefore, on Christmas Day 1956 Tom dumped a tiny infant orang-utan on her bed, to which she was confined by a cold, she was overwhelmed by its eagerness to snuggle into her arms.

'His mother was shot,' said Tom. 'He was found by a forest guard in a long-house. We shall have to look after him for a while.'

Thus began five unremitting years of foster parentage to a succession of orphaned baby orang-utans, to which Barbara and also, whenever his other duties permitted, Tom devoted their energies and gave over their home and garden.

Rearing orang-utan babies is a task every bit as demanding as is the care of human infants; indeed it is more difficult because from birth the orang-utan is far more mobile and inquisitive. Left in a room unattended it will wreck everything movable in five minutes. Barbara learned this the hard way and quickly devised suitable living quarters for little Bob, as she called her first orphan. It was nursed, fed and bathed in the house, but slept and played in a roofed cage constructed between the bathroom and the garden, where it could be supervised through a window. The cage was provided with a swing and climbing ropes, a wide shelf and snug sleeping quarters with a sacking blanket which was treated as a surrogate mother in Barbara's absence. The Land Dyak houseboy Bidai took turns to satisfy Bob's constant demands for cuddling or playing in the garden.

Shortly afterwards a second orphan arrived. It was covered with festering sores, having been chained like a dog beneath the house of a Chinese trader. At first it refused food or drink and was obviously dying, but Barbara nursed it back to health, first force-feeding it with milk from a pipette and then graduating to a baby's bottle, to which it responded eagerly. Three more babies then arrived in quick succession, all of them confiscated from native villages or town traders. One had pneumonia and though rushed to hospital, soon died. The remainder thrived under Barbara's growing expertise. All her waking hours were occupied with the needs of her excessively active brood. Soon the shade-trees in the garden were being denuded of branches to provide fresh foliage with which the young orangs obviously enjoyed playing, or trying to weave into rudimentary nests. No textbook had ever been written about the care or needs of young orangs and she was determined to learn what was best for them. There seemed only one way to do so – to study them in a wild state in the jungle. Having reached this conclusion, she announced that she would make a lengthy expedition into the unexplored rain-forests where orangs were known to occur. Her long-suffering husband and Bidai would have to look after the orphans while she was away.

Barbara was no neophyte when it came to roughing it in the jungle, having already accompanied Tom on archaeological and collecting expeditions. She spoke fluent Malay and had no fear of being alone with Dyaks. To many white women, however, her proposal would have been regarded as foolhardy if not downright dangerous.

To accompany her she chose a reliable Land Dyak to act as cook-handyman and the museum's star collector, Guan Anak Sureng, an Iban Dyak who had served with distinction in the Sarawak Rangers during the long campaign against Communist guerillas in Malaya. He was a crack shot and an expert in jungle craft. Moreover Tom, whose duties prevented him from joining the expedition, trusted him.

The first three days were spent crossing the South China Sea and thence up the river into the Sebuyau district. Next morning, accompanied by a local Iban guide, they began walking in single file into secondary jungle, cutting their way through clinging vines and thorn thickets with their *parangs* and wading muddy streams. By midday they found an abandoned thatched hut on high stilts, which they entered by climbing the usual notched log serving as a stairway. Here they cooked a meal before entering the giant trees of the rain-forest which lay ahead.

Leaving their baggage in the hut they set off again, with Guan walking ahead and marking the trail by bending down twigs or leaves at ten-yard intervals, it being perilously easy to get separated and lost in such surroundings. Several times they saw various monkey species, but no sign of the tell-tale nests of orang-utans. As they began the long walk back to the hut, rain came hissing down like a savage tide, soaking them to the skin. The rain-forest was living up to its name.

During the night Guan shot a civet and Barbara was given its brains with rice for breakfast. Two days later, after an exhausting search, they found their first orang's nest, its leaves still green and obviously fresh. As they approached, a great shaggy body clad in chestnut fur slipped silently from it and disappeared. Guan, like all Dyaks, had a deep respect and sympathy for wild animals. Turning to Barbara he said, 'We have disturbed him in his midday nap. We better not follow but show him our good intentions. He will be in a temper now.' Disappointed, but respecting Guan's opinion, Barbara returned to camp, where they made a meal from a fallen daurian fruit.

The daurian grows throughout the South-East Asian forests and is highly prized by man and beast – even tigers relish it. The golden fruit is as large as a football and covered with short, sharp spikes. Inside is a white juicy flesh and chestnut-size seeds. Falling as much as a hundred feet from the tree, the heavy fruit can break a man's skull. I have never been able to enjoy a daurian because of its overpowering smell, which is like a mixture of rotten eggs and sewage. The trees are widely cultivated, however, and when the fruit is ripe the stench in the markets is overpowering. At weekends city dwellers drive into the country to bring back loads of daurians in their cars, which then smell as though they had been transporting skunks.

Barbara lay huddled under her wet mosquito net that night listening to the noises of the forest – the frogs, crickets, jungle nightjars and owls. At last she was about to realize her ambition to watch wild orang-utans. She desperately wanted to return her orphans to a natural existence and knew that their fixation on human foster parents deprived them of the essential knowledge which only their real parents could impart. How could she teach them to recognize the right wild food sources and how to escape predators? She must learn. She determined to spend as much time as possible perched as high as she could climb up a tree, watching orang-utans.

A few days later, after they had located a group of several new nests, Guan aroused her an hour before sunrise. Wet and shivering, she drank the mug of tea which he brought her and wondered if she was mad to have exchanged the comforts of home for the hardships of jungle life. To attempt to climb a high tree in total darkness was sheer folly, but the thought of her orphans strengthened her resolve. With Guan's help she stumbled through the rain-soaked vegetation to a tree overlooking the nest site. Having climbed as far up as she could, she crawled out along a branch and he lashed her to it securely. Armed with her camera, a notebook and a sharp *parang*, she settled down in the dripping darkness, having instructed Guan to stay away from the area.

Scarcely moving, she remained perched there for six long hours, suffering acutely from arrested circulation and muscular pain. But the spectacle she witnessed was of entrancing interest. Three orang-utans emerged from their nests as the sun rose and throughout the morning held her enthralled by their behaviour. She watched every detail of their morning toilet, how they cleaned their fur and dried it in the sun, how they breakfasted off daurian fruit, tearing them open with their powerful hands and scooping out the juicy pulp, how they cleaned and repaired their nests or built new ones, how they drank water from hollows in the tree trunks or sipped it from hanging orchid flowers, and how they played and showed off to each other. She was the first woman to watch these activities in a wild population and she recorded everything with her camera and notebook.

For three weeks Barbara and her companions lived in the rain-forest, moving from one camp or long-house to another, amassing an invaluable documentation on the orang-utans. She then returned to Kuching to put into practice what she had learned.

Her theories were right, but in practice difficulties were quickly apparent. Some of the young orangs took readily to the garden trees and built nests in them in which they slept, soon establishing a semi-wild existence. Others, however, proved unable to sever their bond with their foster mother, to whom they clung desperately. For such animals, she concluded sadly, there might be no alternative but life in a zoo. But as time passed it became increasingly obvious that the garden had insufficient resources for the now semi-wild orangs, which were steadily destroying all the trees. What was needed was a protected tract of rain-forest, where they could gradually make contact with their own kind, while remaining under skilled supervision. Such a solution demanded a great deal of money and in those days there was no source which could provide it.

The garden a shambles and the number of new orphaned babies still increasing, Barbara was in despair. She found temporary relief by cajoling a neighbour into accepting some of the semi-wild orangs in his large garden, where they settled happily. But her resources were exhausted and it was only compounding her difficulties to continue without the means of returning the animals to the wild. With infinite regret she finally accepted Tom's edict that the captives she had raised must be offered to the few reliable zoos which could look after them properly. After five years of unremitting endeavour, she felt defeated.

Barbara was not defeated, however. During the next five years she played a leading part and indeed was the driving force in the ultimate creation of scientifically managed rehabilitation centres for orphaned young orang-utans, in Sarawak, Sabah, Sumatra and Kalimantan. Funds were by then becoming available for such work, notably from the World Wildlife Fund; so also were qualified scientists who could apply and further develop the expertise which she had initiated. She recognized that her work would have no real future unless the local people understood its value and accepted the responsibility for continuing it without dependence on expatriate assistance. This, too, is now being achieved. Both Malaysia and Indonesia are rapidly developing admirable conservation programmes by their own initiative and already have a number of highly skilled wildlife experts who have earned the respect of visiting scientists from other countries.

Initially the rehabilitation centres were directed by specialists of European or North American origin, assisted by Indonesian or Malaysian students, who showed remarkable aptitude for the work. There are now four of these centres. The first one was created in 1964 by Stanley De Silva in the Sepilok Forest Reserve in Sabah. Herman Rijksen and his wife made one at Ketambe in 1971, in the Sumatran province of Aceh. In 1972 the Canadians Rod and Birute Galdikas-Brindamour opened one in the Tanjung Puting Reserve in Kalimantan. Monica Borner-Loewensberg and Dr Regina Frey from Switzerland have managed the Bohorok Rehabilitation Centre at Langkat, in Sumatra's Gunung Leuser Reserve, since 1972. It is hoped that another new one will soon be established in Sarawak. Although contributing to the survival of the species by returning captives to the wild (more than fifty have already been successfully released), the chief importance of the centres is their educational value. They help to convince the local people of the value of the orang-utan and the paramount need to prevent the destruction of its forest habitat, which has now become the primary factor in its survival.

The work of Barbara Harrisson was heroic and of value both to science and to the zoos of the world, many of which paid tribute to her skill. It was also invaluable to those who later took her ambitions to final fruition. Dr Tom Harrisson, alas, was killed in a bus crash in Thailand in 1975. He had been Chairman of the Primates Group at the IUCN and his name was added to the Roll of Honour which the World Wildlife Fund maintains to commemorate the work of great naturalists. Barbara's book will also remain as a classic of natural history and personal endeavour.

By the time John MacKinnon began his work on orang-utans in 1968 their number had declined greatly. The populations which survived were now even more threatened by the ruthless onslaught of forest exploitation by the Japanese, North American and European timber companies. The rain-forests of the world were disappearing and it was said that in thirty years none would be left.* Everywhere the orang-utan was now an officially protected species, but its habitat was steadily shrinking. The illegal capture of baby orangs continued, though most of them now had some chance of survival in the rehabilitation reserves if confiscated in time.

John was born in 1947 and educated at Winchester and Oxford, where he read zoology. After spending a year studying chimpanzees with Jane Goodall and Hugo van Lawick in Tanzania's Gombe Reserve, he decided on a one-man expedition to learn about orang-utans. Chimpanzees had been relatively easy, but orangs were solitary, living in inaccessible rain-forests. It seemed logical to him, therefore, that the only way to study them was literally to live with

*The WWF has seventy projects concerned with the preservation of sample areas in Asia, Africa and South America, but at present only 2 per cent of of the world's rain-forests are protected.

C

them, to sleep where they slept and to follow them wherever they went, if necessary for months on end. That this had never yet been attempted on the scale he intended added the kind of challenge which appealed to him.

John MacKinnon wrote a remarkable book about his subsequent adventures.* In the foreword, David Attenborough, who had personal experience of life in the rainforests, wrote of him,

It is only such a man who can – either by design, or even more dangerously by accident – get close enough to a forest elephant to provoke its charge. And only someone as stoically hardy as he would make his bed in the regular path of a porcupine, simply because an ape had chosen to go to sleep in the branches a hundred feet above that particular spot.

Many more adventures than these befell MacKinnon during the following two years in Sabah and Sumatra.

As Indonesia and Sarawak were only just recovering from the recent revolution, he chose Sabah for his first expedition. Orang-utans were still relatively plentiful in the hill-forests around its eastern rivers. Armed with a Malay grammar, a camera, a box of tropical medicines and the absolute minimum of creature comforts, he set out for the Ulu Segama Reserve, an area of some 600 square miles of virgin rainforest as yet unexplored by any qualified zoologist. He had never set eyes on a wild orang and had little idea of what was in store for him.

He landed on the coast at Sandakan, where he discussed his plans with the game warden. The reserve could be reached only by way of the treacherous Segama River. But first he wanted to visit the orang-utan rehabilitation centre, which the game warden, Stanley De Silva, had set up in the nearby Sepilok Reserve. There, as far as possible from human contact, confiscated young orangs were first fed, doctored and sheltered and then allowed to wander at will. Very soon they learned to follow the more experienced animals into the jungle and to gain experience in the skills of

*MacKinnon, John, *In Search of the Red Ape*, Collins, London, 1974.

survival. Those which had difficulty in breaking their dependence on man were carried pick-a-back by wardens and
released in the forest, to find their own way back to the feeding station. The system worked and already many were
joining their wild companions. John was fascinated by what
he saw.

Next day he flew south to Lahad Datu, where he hired a
small *sampan* and two Dusun natives to take him up the
Segama River. An obliging Chinese geologist offered to take
him in his fast outboard launch, leaving the *sampan* to follow,
but he was full of forebodings about the maniac idea of living
alone in the jungle among dangerous wild animals, such as
sun bears, which had recently killed two men. MacKinnon,
unimpressed, accepted his offer.

The journey up-river was a spectacular introduction to the
wilds of Sabah. Many species of monkeys roamed the tree-
tops and there were hosts of colourful birds such as kingfishers and hornbills, to say nothing of a colony of huge
fox-bats. The party camped on an island that night and at
sunrise, after breakfasting on a mouse deer shot by one of the
boatmen, continued their journey. At midday they reached
the junction of the Segama and Bole rivers, where they were
to part. The boatmen built a shelter for MacKinnon and
after showing him which vines provided drinking water and
which plants were poisonous, left him to await the slow
sampan, which would arrive several days later. He was now
alone in the dense jungle.

His first day alone would have scared a lesser man.
Although experienced in the African bush, he was new to the
tropical rain-forest. The immense height and density of its
vegetation, with its ever-present sharply hooked vines,
stinging plants and myriads of strange insects frustrated him.
Nevertheless, with the aid of a compass, he explored his
surroundings, hacking his way into the vegetation, which at
times he had to crawl through. Very quickly he learned that
all such forests are alive with millions of voracious leeches
and within an hour his arms and legs were bleeding pro-
fusely. I learned in Burma and Malaya that there is no way

of avoiding these loathsome pests and that unless a lighted cigarette or a rag soaked in salt is applied to make them release their suckers they leave a festering sore if pulled off. MacKinnon, too, learned to carry a salt pad wherever he went thereafter.

On his very first exploration he discovered nests of orangutans, which did much to restore his flagging spirits. He also found fresh elephant droppings and the tracks of many animals, including clouded leopard, to add to his excitement. Returning to camp, he refreshed himself with a swim in the river and turned in for his first night in the forest. Ignoring the sandflies and mosquitoes, he slept soundly. Next day he found his first orangs and watched them until dark. He was becoming accustomed to the jungle and spent the whole of the following day quietly moving wherever the orangs went. Initially they were nervous of his presence and occasionally showed their displeasure by throwing branches at him, but gradually they accepted him as harmless. Finding himself very far from the river at dusk, he bedded down below the tree in which the orangs had their nests. A pile of leaves between the high buttresses of a giant tree provided a comfortable bed, with a plastic raincoat to keep off the dew. As a precaution against prowlers he strung a thorny vine between the buttresses. Around him in the inky darkness he became aware of hundreds of tiny, glowing lights, blue, green and yellow, coming from fireflies, fungi and a crawling grub, which carried 'a row of glowing spots along its sides, giving the appearance of a miniature train chugging slowly through the night'. At sunrise he continued his observations.

Having satisfied himself that he could sleep in relative safety in the forest, he adopted this routine in order to spend the maximum time with his subjects. All he needed was to carry sufficient food, which he could supplement with wild fruit. Returning to camp he found that the *sampan* had arrived and that his two Dusuns had erected a more substantial stilted hut, with a store room. They had been alarmed by his absence and were horrified to learn that he had been sleeping unprotected in the jungle.

The next few days passed pleasantly, orang-watching alternating with fishing or hunting wild pigs for the pot. After a torrential storm he woke one morning to find that the river had risen alarmingly and that the stilted hut was now standing in the water. Another spell of sleeping in the forest followed and he got almost within arm's length of one of the orangs. One night he was awakened by a large porcupine running into his foot. He kicked out blindly in the darkness and with the aid of a torch saw the angry animal, quills erect, rushing at him. He stepped aside and it brushed past him. A much more frightening experience occurred later, when a roaming elephant approached in the darkness. He had not realized that he was sleeping on an established animal track. Grabbing his belongings, he retreated, but the elephant had caught his scent and followed closely. Panicking, MacKinnon began to run. Not daring to use his torch, he blundered through the wickedly enveloping hooked *rotan* palm tendrils, tearing his flesh until he collapsed behind a buttressed tree. The elephant crashed past without locating him. The experience unnerved him and for several days he did not enter the forest again.

As the weeks passed he perfected his techniques. A party of visiting Dusuns provided some strong polythene with which he made an easily portable ground-sheet and overhead shelter, thus making his nights in the rain-forest much more comfortable. But his life was spartan, with no radio, no books and only the barest necessities for food. His notebooks were bulging with detailed observations about the behaviour of twenty different orang-utans which he had followed for many days, ranging from old bachelor males to mothers with new-born young.

For three days he was laid low with fever, but returned to his work with a high temperature. He was turning for home when suddenly confronted with the biggest and blackest male orang he had ever seen. It was approaching him on the ground and looked aggressive. Too weak to run, he dived for cover and the great beast ambled past within a few feet. Fascinated by its size and gorilla-like appearance, he foolishly followed it, but could not keep pace. In a few minutes, his head swimming with nausea, he almost ran into it. Fortunately it was more scared than he was and moved away. Too weak to follow, he dragged himself back to camp, where he collapsed, wondering vaguely how he could get to a doctor. He took what medicides he thought appropriate and after a night of delirium felt sufficiently recovered to return to the forest for another day's work. He was a remarkably tough young man.

He had another adventure at night. Although his Malay was improving by conversation with his Dusun boatmen, it was far from perfect and this led to a misunderstanding. He asked them to take him a mile up the Bole River and to return in three hours, but the men mistook this to mean at three o'clock the following day. When they failed to arrive he waited until dark and then decided to swim back to camp. He had scarcely entered the water when he heard a loud splash which he took to have been made by a pursuing crocodile, of which there were many in the river. In inky darkness he scrambled into the branches of an overhanging tree, but hearing nothing further, dropped back into the river and resumed his swim. As he approached the junction of the Bole and the Segama, he was caught in a powerful current which he knew led to a big whirlpool. Only with the utmost effort did he reach the shore, where he continued on foot. When he reached camp the Dusuns upbraided him for his foolishness, but thereafter always referred to him as their *tuan berhani* (fearless master).

Having compiled several hundred hours of observations on orang-utans, MacKinnon returned to Oxford and took the finals for his degree. He also obtained a Leverhulme Scholarship from the Royal Society, which enabled him to continue his studies of the species. Exactly one year after leaving the Segama River he was once more in a *sampan* heading up-river. This time he would be working through the winter monsoon and he came better equipped. Experience had taught him wisdom and he brought with him the luxuries of a camp bed, mosquito netting and portable radio.

Arriving at his old camp site, he found his previous trails still visible and resumed his old routine with the orang-utans. As the season advanced, violent storms beat down on the forest, sending great trees crashing to the ground. One fell almost on top of his canoe, swamping it completely. The orangs hated the storms and roared loudly at each onslaught.

His knowledge of the rain-forest and of living on its resources was by now extensive. He no longer experienced fear but felt at home, recognizing everything he saw and knowing its value. For example, now even the hated leeches could serve him as both bait and hook for fishes – if one was tied to the tendril of a creeper and lowered into the water, any fish which tried to eat it was instantly secured by the leech's sucker and could be pulled to the surface. He ate many unaccustomed foods, such as monitor lizards, tortoises and various fungi. The fame of his medicine box spread far and wide. When one of his Dusuns was carried into the camp severely gored by a wild pig, MacKinnon was confidently expected to save his life. After drugging him with morphia, he stitched up the huge wound with an ordinary sewing needle and a nylon thread extracted from a piece of rope. When the patient miraculously recovered, MacKinnon's reputation again soared. It soared even further when, having been bitten by a python, he assured them that he would suffer no ill effects. There are thirty species of poisonous snakes in Borneo, but the python is not one of them – it kills by crushing its prey. All snakes were poisonous to the Dusun. Finally MacKinnon miraculously survived an attack by a furious sun bear, whose raking claws missed him by inches. So impressed were his men that they promised, if and when he ever died, they would bury him with the full ceremonials accorded to a true Dusun.

Throughout his 1970 expedition to Sabah MacKinnon continued his intensive study of orang-utans. He then wrote his doctoral thesis under Professor Niko Tinbergen and Dr Desmond Morris. The following year he obtained a grant from the Science Research Council to visit Sumatra in order to continue his studies. He began work in the West

Langkat Reserve, to the east of the famous and much larger Gunung Leuser Reserve, which lies on the opposite bank of the Alas River. The Indonesian scene was new to him and the Bornean Malay which he now spoke fluently was barely comprehensible to the local people. Nevertheless he rapidly settled into his familiar routine and on arrival at his first camp was greeted by the bellowing cries of Sumatran orangs which were engaged in mating, a function he had not witnessed in Sabah.

After a spell in this area he journeyed back to the coast and prepared for a long stay in the Gunung Leuser Reserve. An agonizing journey of ten hours in an overcrowded native bus, jammed with passengers, livestock and baskets of fruit, brought him near its border, only to find that he would require both a jeep and a boat in order to complete the distance. Having the funds for neither of these luxuries, he set off on foot to explore the huge forest on the reserve boundary. The country here is mountainous and crisscrossed with streams and waterfalls, but by following elephant trails he made good progress, eventually finding an ideal site for a base camp. This was an abandoned hut by a big waterfall, where Rajah Brooke bird-wing butterflies sailed on six-inch wings of shining green and black. Siamang gibbons were barking in the adjacent trees and there were orang-utan nests near by. He was soon happily settled to his work of observing, writing, photographing and filming. Only the presence of elephants, tigers and leopards prevented him from sleeping out with his subjects.

After several weeks of this idyllic existence, news reached him that his fiancée Kathy was coming from England to join him. He hurried back to Medan and thence to Singapore to meet her. To his consternation she arrived complete with white bridal dress and wedding cake, whereas he had nothing but his tattered bush clothes. After hastily buying a suit, a tie and shoes, the young couple reached Sumatra, where they went through an Indonesian marriage ceremony, of which Kathy did not understand a single word. This was followed by an English-style wedding at the British Consulate and a riotous feast at a friend's house, to the accompaniment of authentic Scottish bagpipes and the cutting of the wedding cake with a Malayan *kris*. The happy pair then set out for the camp in a World Wildlife Fund Land-Rover, trailing strings of tin cans in the traditional manner. With them went a baby leopard cat and a sick baby orang-utan, as an introduction to the kind of life Kathy would henceforth lead.

Kathy is a very pretty girl with an elfin expression. She must have been very much in love to have put up with what followed. After a very long, hot journey they reached the point where the road petered out and then faced a nine-mile walk, carrying their baggage through muddy paddyfields and banana plantations. It was a singular journey for a young bride fresh from England, but they finally reached the river, which they crossed by dugout canoe, and arrived at the camp. Here an ever-increasing crowd of native villagers assembled to inspect the newly-weds. They had obviously come for an evening's entertainment. Nothing would move them, so the embarrassed MacKinnon and his bride had no option but to bed down for the night on a palm mat, surrounded by nudging and giggling men, women and children. Hours passed before the crowd drifted away and sleep became possible.

It was a strange beginning to a honeymoon, but as the months passed Kathy settled into John's routine and thoroughly enjoyed sharing his work in the ever-changing scene of wildlife and jungle, for she, too, was a trained zoologist completing her thesis.

John MacKinnon's work on the orang-utan greatly advanced scientific knowledge of the species. Barbara Harrisson had shown that miserably orphaned young could be successfully raised to healthy maturity and, with care, could be returned to the wild. MacKinnon revealed in greater depth the secrets of the behaviour of the wild population and their ecological requirements. These two and others have provided the essential knowledge on which effective conservation measures can be planned. There is, however, still much to be learned about orang-utans, for, as Barbara

Harrisson has pointed out, the harvesting of results from research takes much longer with this species than with the gorilla or chimpanzee. Nevertheless, the surviving wild and semi-wild populations of orang-utans are better managed than ever before. They are still an endangered species, but the number of protected reserves created for them by the Indonesian and Malaysian authorities is steadily increasing.

The total number of wild orangs probably now exceeds 15000, and they have been saved from the threat of extinction which in the 1950s seemed inevitable. To Barbara Harrisson, John MacKinnon and the pioneer workers at the rehabilitation centres, the world is deeply indebted.

Barbara now has an important position in the Department of Asian Studies at the West Australian Institute of Technology. When I last heard of the MacKinnons they were living in a tiny native hut in a remote forest in Sulawesi, working on a new research project. A wild boar had recently attacked their four-year-old son; John, as usual unarmed, had had a finger bitten off while rescuing him. The price paid for our knowledge of wildlife can sometimes by a very heavy one.

5

THE CRADLE OF EVOLUTION

IT was September 1835. Charles Darwin, at the age of twenty-four, his mind still full of the splendours of the South American tropics, stood on the deck of HMS *Beagle* gazing at an island the like of which he had never seen before. Its surface was black and menacing, humped with volcanic strata, out of which sprouted the jagged cones of long-extinct blow-holes and crumbling, petrified bubbles of lava. Here and there rose the gaunt stem of an opuntia or brachycereus cactus. At a distance the island appeared like a lifeless moonscape. Indeed, as he confided in his journal, the 'strange Cyclopean scene' looked and smelled like what he imagined 'the infernal regions' to be. Robert FitzRoy, captain of the *Beagle*, feeling equally disconcerted, described it as 'a shore fit for pandemonium'.

This was Chatham Island, the first island of the Galápagos archipelago one normally sees after sailing due west along the Equator for 600 miles into the Pacific from Guayaquil, in Ecuador. I have made this exciting journey three times and once each from Peru and Panama.

When Darwin landed on the black sand in St Stephen's Harbour he noted that it was hot enough to burn his feet through the soles of his boots. But what immediately excited him was to find the island inhabited by animals entirely new to him. Most extraordinary were the truly enormous tortoises which slowly ambled without the least sign of fear among the sailors. He measured one and found it eight feet around its middle, with a weight of about 500 pounds. The beach was littered with the empty carapaces of tortoises killed by the crews of passing whalers and privateers, and with the stretchers on which others had been carried to be stored alive on board. They made a welcome substitute for the weevil-infested salt pork which was the usual fare for sailors. Hundreds of thousands of these innocent monsters had perished in this manner.

Darwin was also surprised to find two different kinds of iguanas on the Galápagos Islands, neither of which he had seen in South America. One lived in burrows and, like the giant tortoises, ate the fleshy leaves of opuntia cacti; it was buffish in colour and grew to more than three feet in length.

The other, black and crested from head to tail, lived among the black coastal rocks and swam in the surf. He later discovered that it fed on algae and seaweed on the sea bed – which was incredible behaviour for any reptile. There were some very strange little finch-like birds, too, drab and brown or black, with bills of very different sizes. Little wine-red doves with blue eyes settled confidently on his head and shoulders, or took food from his hand. It was all very bewildering and unbelievable. All the animals were so tame! Collecting specimens was a simple matter of knocking them on the head with a stick.

For five weeks the *Beagle* sailed from island to island. The archipelago extends for 150 miles westward and is spread over an area of 3000 square miles. Darwin did not have time to visit even all the larger islands, but he spent a week camped on James Island, where he collected another twenty-six species of birds new to him. Their complete tameness continued to fascinate yet worry him. 'We may infer', he wrote, 'what havoc the introduction of any new beast of prey must cause in a country before the instincts of the indigenous inhabitants have become adapted to the stranger's craft and power.' These were prophetic words. He little knew what was to happen to the Galápagos a hundred years later.

The collection of specimens of unique animals and plants

which Darwin made was extremely important, though far from complete. He longed to add to it, but the *Beagle* could not linger and headed westward towards the distant Society Islands in mid-Pacific.

Back in his cabin Darwin pondered over his specimens. It was immediately apparent that there were distinct differences between the lava lizards, finches, iguanas and giant tortoises from different islands, though within each group there were obvious relationships. How could this be? The islands were only a few hours' sailing from each other, yet the lizards and iguanas had different colourations and the bills of the little finches varied greatly in form and size. Was each a different species? Could such differences exist within a single species? Here was a mockingbird from Chatham Island with a short bill, yet on Hood Island, only thirty miles away, there was one with a bill twice the length. Why should the giant tortoise from Indefatigable Island have a round, domed carapace, while those on Duncan be upturned in front, like a Spanish saddle? His mind buzzed with speculation. Again and again he turned to the finches. There could be no doubt, he decided, that they belonged to the same family, though their bills varied from one as small and almost as fine as a warbler's, to one as deep and massive as a hawfinch's. Could it be that one species had colonized all the islands and in the course of time had changed into such remarkable variations? The thought was shattering in its implications and led to disturbing doubts about the firmly held contemporary belief in the origins of all life on earth. Like all Victorians, Darwin had been brought up convinced of the infallibility of the Book of Genesis, which declared that all creatures, including man, had been created intact in their present form by God. Nevertheless, his studies of fossil remains of long-extinct giant animals which he had found in South America had already caused him grave misgivings, which he had confided to nobody. Now his mind was in turmoil; yet so powerful was the influence of his upbringing that he dared not commit his thoughts to paper. Only ten years later could he find the courage to write cautiously in his journal, concerning the

Galápagos finches, 'Seeing the graduation and diversity of structure in one small, intimately related group of birds, one might really fancy that, from an original paucity of birds in the archipelago, one species had been taken and modified for different ends.' Even to go this far was to deny the Biblical concept of creation.

It is doubtful if Darwin would ever have summoned the courage publicly to go further had it not been for his contemporary, Alfred Russel Wallace. Working on the other side of the world in the Malay archipelago, Wallace had reached conclusions similar to Darwin's, pointing to evolution by natural selection. Darwin was astounded when Wallace's letter reached him and finally agreed that their joint findings should be presented at a meeting of the Linnaean Society in London. Thus, twenty-two years after his visit to the Galápagos, the theory of evolution was made public. The following year Darwin's *Origin of Species* burst like a bombshell on the unsuspecting world. The entire first edition was sold out on the first day and uproar ensued. This long and scholarly work and his later *Descent of Man* resulted in theological controversy of a violence impossible to imagine today. Darwin was denounced from the pulpit, reviled in the press and lampooned in the music-halls. A sense of blasphemy and outrage prevailed. But the door had been opened to man's knowledge of the universe and there was no closing it. In spite of the thundering of the Church, the belief that Adam and Eve had been created in the Garden of Eden was gradually replaced by knowledge that man was descended by the long process of evolution from primitive animal ancestors. At a stroke human history was stripped of its cloying mythology. What Darwin had learned in the Galápagos provided the solid basis on which all evolutionary biology and genetics have since been built.

The Spanish called the Galápagos 'Las Islas Incantadas' – the enchanted islands. Though at a distance they appear forbidding, once one steps ashore they are indeed enchanting, even to those not scientifically minded. In geological terms they are of only recent origin, being the crests of submarine volcanoes which erupted from the floor of the Pacific a million or so years ago. Occasionally there is still volcanic activity and I was present to see the beginning of a very violent outbreak on the island of Fernandina in 1968. The eruption continued for a whole month, by which time the floor of the caldera had sunk by 1000 feet and a lake which had been at one end had moved to the opposite side.

Galápago is the Spanish word for tortoise and it was only the prospect of obtaining these animals for food which attracted ships to these inhospitable islands. The original discoverer was Fray Tomas de Berlenga, Bishop of Panama, who in 1535 described them as 'looking as though God had caused it to rain stones'. Finding no water there, he was reduced to chewing cactus leaves to quench his thirst. Water sources are indeed very scarce and are absent on most of the islands. The British named them individually in the seventeenth century. They were then taken by Spain and in 1832 by Ecuador, who re-named them, giving each a name associated with Christopher Columbus, though he had never set foot on them. Today, confusingly, they still have both English and Ecuadorian names. Various attempts to colonize them, including the forced settlement of convicts, soon failed for lack of water; but eventually a small mixed population contrived to live on the few islands where it was available. They were mostly ship-wrecked pirates, or fugitives from the law. Murder was commonplace and cannibalism not unknown. Even in more recent times the population has been of mixed nationalities with little respect for law or the niceties of social behaviour. Many inhabitants have disappeared without trace, their bodies being easily disposed of in the deep fissures of the lava wilderness. One of the strangest of the moderns was the 'mad' Baroness Eloisa Bosquet von Wagner, who settled on Floreana in 1932 with three boyfriends who subsequently disappeared in very mysterious circumstances. I recall meeting another entertaining character, a swashbuckling, white-bearded and pot-bellied citizen of Alsace, who was reputed to play havoc with the local girls on Santa Cruz. When HRH Prince Philip visited the

Galápagos, this gay old scoundrel greeted him on the quay stark naked.

From the 1920s onward the population of the Galápagos began to increase rapidly and has now risen to 5000, though it still has to depend on the far-distant mainland for everything except fish and the little food raised in the moist highlands. The spread of irrigation and agriculture, the destruction of the highland sunflower-tree forest* and the increase in buildings are causing deep concern for the wildlife. Many South American plants have been introduced, which are speedily replacing the unique native vegetation. With them have come invasive alien insects such as the extremely harmful *Wasmannia* fire-ant. During the past hundred years settlers have introduced goats, pigs, donkeys, cattle, dogs, cats and, of course, rats on many of the islands. These scourges to island ecosystems multiplied to enormous numbers, destroying the vegetation and preying on the native fauna to such an extent as to exterminate some species completely. Goats, dogs and cats in a feral state are exceptionally difficult to eradicate in such terrain and rats virtually impossible.

The next threat began innocently enough, when Lars Eric Lindblad, the pioneer of sophisticated natural history tours, landed the first small group of tourists on the Galápagos. Being himself a conservationist, he took steps to make sure that the wildlife was not disturbed and that all litter was removed. Unfortunately pioneers are quickly imitated. The glowing accounts brought back by the Lindblad tourists spread like wildfire and before long many much less responsible 'package tours' to the Galápagos were organized by rival companies of different nationalities. Soon the annual influx of tourists rose to thousands (there were 9000 in 1977) and the disturbance to wildlife became a serious matter. Seabirds were kept off their nests, enabling predators to take their eggs, vegetation was trampled and litter abounded. The breeding success of several rare species declined sharply.

Fortunately the government of Ecuador has now turned the whole archipelago, apart from already settled areas, into

* An endemic composite of the genus Scalesia.

An adult male orang-utan has large, fleshy pouches around its face. Destruction of the Indonesian rain-forests now threatens the survival of the species.

The Charles Darwin Foundation saved the Galápagos giant tortoises by hatching their eggs in incubators to prevent their destruction by rats and other predators.

The waved albatross is unique to the Galápagos. Its courtship is an elaborate combination of bowing, gaping, bill-clattering and braying like a donkey.

The survival of the
flightless giant
pied-billed grebe
of Lake Atitlán was
due to several
lonely years of
devoted work by
Anne La Bastille.

This unique bird is
found only at Lake
Atitlán in Guatemala,
where its habitat
was threatened by
touristic
developments, reed-
cutters and a huge
hydro-electric
project.

The deeply eroded coral 'mushrooms' in the lagoon on the remote island of Aldabra provided ideal resting and nesting sites for various seabirds.

Hundreds of giant tortoises of the Indian Ocean race were sheltering from the blistering sun beneath the stunted trees as we stepped ashore on Aldabra.

a national park and has introduced regulations limiting
tourists to marked trails on the vulnerable islands. But the
penalties of tourism cannot be completely removed. It is
entirely proper that the world should be enabled to enjoy the
wonders of the Galápagos and this brings important revenue,
though scientists would prefer that the islands should be
isolated from all human disturbance. Although tourists are
now not permitted to approach nesting birds closely, their
presence is still a hazard. The unique Galápagos albatross
may remain apparently undisturbed on its egg, but experiments have shown that if a microphone is placed in its nest
its heart-beat doubles at the sight of a human being approaching, even at what is thought to be a 'safe' distance. The
unintentional interruption of courtship or of feeding nestlings
can seriously affect breeding success. Moreover, behaviour
patterns are changing and research workers can no longer
be certain that they are studying truly natural life cycles.

The wildlife of the Galápagos has been evolved over a
period of a million years or more, hitherto in almost complete
isolation. This isolation from the stabilizing influence of a
constant genetic interchange such as occurs in a continental
land-mass has encouraged the creation of new species. The
original bird and reptile colonists were free to experiment
and occupy ecological niches which on the mainland were
chosen by other species. In the absence of competitors, those
which succeeded in adapting to the new environment were
free to evolve new feeding behaviour and to develop in a
direction most suited to their new existence.

The reptilean colonists reached the islands by riding on
rafts of vegetation carried out to sea from the rivers of the
mainland. The original finches were doubtless gale-drifted
from the South American coast. Those which were most
adaptable survived in the alien surroundings by taking
advantage of whatever food and shelter they could find. If
food could be found by probing the flowers of cacti, some of
them began to specialize in this behaviour. Those with the
longest bills were most likely to succeed and to reproduce.
For others, perhaps on different islands, the habit of feeding

on hard seeds gradually led, by natural selection, to the development of heavier bills and more powerful jaw muscles. The distances between the islands helped this specialization. Eventually the changes became so marked and the behaviour so specialized that new species were evolved, that is to say that the populations separated ecologically and physiologically and no longer interbred. This process is still continuing and one can detect hybrid forms between some of the closely related seed-eating finches which have evidently not yet completely separated.

Apart from the various seed-eaters and the cactus finch, there is one that acts like a typical insectivorous warbler, one that turns over stones fifteen times its own weight to find food, another which fills the ecological niche of the absent woodpeckers but, lacking the long tongue of a woodpecker, holds the spine of a cactus in its bill to dig for grubs in dead wood. As recently as 1964 it was discovered that yet another species of finch had developed the vampire-like habit of taking blood from the bases of flight-feathers of nesting boobies – a truly extraordinary initiative which may yet lead to it becoming a miniature carnivore.

By similar processes of isolation and natural selection, each island now has its own distinct and colourful lava lizard. The different giant tortoises and iguanas have already been mentioned. Of birds, 127 species have been recorded. Fifty-seven of these are resident and no fewer than twenty-eight are unique to the Galápagos. The variety of species is explained by the fact that although many islands are low and arid, others have volcanic peaks high enough to attract clouds and vegetation; the mountain of Isabela rises to 5600 feet and has a verdant tropical forest not unlike some to be found on the Ecuadorian mainland. The unique bird species are the flightless cormorant, the miniature penguin (living on the Equator!), the albatross, the lava heron, the black lava gull, the very beautiful swallowtailed gull, the so-called Galápagos hawk (which is actually a buzzard with extremely variable plumage), the dove, the rail, the large-billed flycatcher, the martin, the four different mockingbirds and, of course, the thirteen famous finches. To tourists, the most popular birds are the huge frigatebirds and the three species of boobies, which nest in vast colonies along the shores and feed in the ocean. The marine life is exceptionally rich, thanks to the copious plankton which the cold Humboldt Current carries through the islands. Sealions in hundreds occupy the sheltered bays and there are small colonies of fur seals on some islands. Whales, dolphins, sharks and giant manta rays abound in the off-shore waters.

Of all the wild inhabitants of the Galápagos, I would choose the albatross as the most fascinating to watch. Large numbers nest on Hood Island. In flight they demonstrate a complete mastery of their element, gliding and banking effortlessly for thousands of miles over the ocean on their long narrow wings, which have a spread of eight feet. Almost their entire lives are spent in flight and when they return to their breeding grounds they are hopelessly handicapped for their brief terrestrial sojourn. When they land on Hood, it is often by crash-landing and up-ending. They walk very slowly, with a ponderous, waddling gait, like over-fed geese, with frequent pauses to rest. But their courtship is an unforgettable spectacle which is repeated again and again each time the pair meets at the nest site. The two great birds stand almost breast to breast, bowing deeply, rocking from side to side, opening their enormous yellow bills to the fullest extent and snapping them shut, fencing with their bills and clattering them together with a noise like machine-gun fire and braying like donkeys with their bills pointed vertically on outstretched necks. These elaborate ceremonies obviously give them unbounded pleasure. Unfortunately the albatrosses are not very intelligent. I have twice seen one settle beside its egg instead of on it, whereupon the watchful mockingbirds quickly swooped on the exposed egg, punctured it and ate the contents. The sitting albatross scarcely bothered to turn its head to watch the commotion only inches from its flank. On another occasion all the albatrosses deserted their eggs because of the torment caused by a sudden enormous outbreak of mosquitoes on Hood, which covered the sitting birds like a sooty blanket. Because the Galápagos albatross breeds nowhere else in the world, a complete failure such as this was a serious matter.

In 1957, as the multiple threats to the Galápagos became more apparent, several missions under the aegis of UNESCO and IUCN began, with the co-operation of the government of Ecuador, to study the means of protecting the unique fauna and flora. In 1959 the Charles Darwin Foundation for the Galápagos was created by a group of distinguished scientists, among whom Sir Julian Huxley, Professor Eibl-Eibesfeldt and Professor Roger Heim were prominent. As its first Director they chose Professor Victor Van Straelen, who devoted the remainder of his life to saving the Galápagos. It was largely by his inspiration that in 1960 the Charles Darwin Research Station was established on the island of Santa Cruz. Here a small resident staff and visiting scientists were able to begin the long task of studying all aspects of the natural history of the archipelago and of planning its conservation. With financial assistance from the World Wildlife Fund and other institutions in the United States and Europe it has made censuses of the endangered wildlife and conducted research ranging from volcanology to micro-biology. Its steady outflow of publications has been of great value to science.

The station had its own modest research vessel, *Beagle II.* When this was worn out, the World Wildlife Fund found a generous donor who provided a replacement. *Beagle III* now plies the dangerous seas between the islands, carrying eager young research workers on their various assignments. There is a formal agreement between the Minister of Foreign Affairs for the Republic of Ecuador and the Foundation, authorizing the latter to act in an advisory capacity concerning conservation. This collaboration has proved cordial and fruitful. The station has neither the authority nor the manpower to police the islands, but since they were declared a national park they are patrolled by forty-eight Ecuadorian wardens trained by the station staff in wildlife management. All tourist ships now have a licensed guide on board. The organized hunting of feral domestic animals is constant and it provides a useful supplement of meat for the local population. Tens of thousands of harmful pests, including 41 000 goats, have thus been removed, though it will be many years before satisfactory levels can be established. Gradually, though always desperately short of funds, the station is improving the conservation of the islands and educating the islanders and tourists to respect the wildlife.

Among the most important achievements of the Charles Darwin Station has been its work on the giant tortoises, which have always been particularly vulnerable. Some of the species were already extinct, killed off by ships' crews. All the remainder had suffered severely from the feral animals which had destroyed their habitat, preyed on their young, or eaten their eggs. The giant tortoise unique to Duncan Island, for example, had not bred successfully for thirty years, all its eggs having been destroyed by rats. Experimentally a clutch of its eggs was taken to the laboratory and hatched in an incubator, the young then being moved to protected pens. As they apparently thrived, the decision was taken to remove all the eggs laid on Duncan as soon as they appeared and a battery of special equipment was constructed for hatching them and raising the young. As soon as the exact temperature and humidity required were learned, the rate of success was very high. As it proved impossible to eradicate the rats on Duncan with traps in the labyrinth of lava, or to use poison without endangering other wildlife, the young tortoises were kept in protected pens until they grew to about one foot in length. At this age they were capable of resisting attack by rats and were then carefully released on their native island. By this means, between 1970 and 1976, the population of a race of giant tortoises which had apparently been heading for certain extinction was saved. By 1976 its tiny population had been increased to 260. All the endangered giant tortoises are now being similarly treated, with the exception of the race on the island of Pinta, which predators have reduced to a single survivor known as 'Lonesome George', an old male which now has no chance of perpetuating its kind. In all, a total of more than 600 young tortoises of ten subspecies have been raised in captivity by the station.

Nowhere in the world is there anything quite like the Galápagos. Nowhere where birds and other animals treat you so trustingly, as though you were a passing friend. Nowhere where the evidence of the evolutionary process is so obvious or so dramatic. Here prehistoric monsters walk in surroundings which make one think of the birth of the universe. There is a magic quality about the behaviour of the wild inhabitants. Where else, as you land, do sealions swim out to poke their shining heads over the gunwale of your boat to greet you, or play tag with you when you go swimming? Where else do birds play with your shoelaces or pull hair from your head to line their nests? I find all this strangely humbling. The trifling work I have done on the Council of the Charles Darwin Foundation has been totally inadequate repayment for the joy the islands have given me.

Ecuador is not a wealthy nation. It is doing its best to protect the Galápagos, of which it is rightly proud. Many scientific institutions in other countries have contributed funds for this task and the World Wildlife Fund has already supported Galápagos projects to the tune of £300000. But the problems of conservation do not diminish with the passage of time. It should not be left to a single government or to hard-pressed charities to protect and restore the birth-place of evolutionary science. The Galápagos Islands represent a fitting international memorial to the genius of Darwin and to man's escape from the shadows of his origins and place in the universe. They are a world heritage, in which every country has an interest, which it should be willing to demonstrate. One day, I hope soon, the United Nations will recognize this.

6

OPERATION POC

BENEATH the 11 600-foot black volcanic peak of Atitlán and the lower peaks of Tolimán and San Pedro, the surface of Lake Atitlán gleamed like burnished steel where the setting moon illuminated it. Near the far shore lay a small open boat in the darkness by a reed-bed, its single occupant hunched immobile in the stern. It was a cold night and the silence was absolute.

Suddenly a weird, strident series of cries echoed across the water, 'caow, caow, *caow-uh, caow-uh*!' Almost immediately it was answered, but this time the sound came from the boat. Then again the cries rang out, but, like the first outburst, they seemed to come from somewhere in the reed-bed.

The first and third calls had been uttered by one of the rarest birds in the world – the giant pied-billed grebe of Guatemala. The second was a tape recording of the voice, played back by Anne La Bastille, the lonely figure in the boat on Lake Atitlán. She was making a census of the grebes, which, being highly territorial by nature, responded readily to this stimulus and thereby revealed their numbers. Challenging them at night when the moon shone gave the best results.

I first met Anne La Bastille in 1962, when my wife and I were visiting the beautiful Adirondack Park in northern New York State. We stayed a weekend at a log-built lodge overlooking Big Moose Lake. It was a site to delight any natura-

list. From the verandah in the early morning we could watch
loons (in Britain we call them great northern divers) on the
misty lake and hear their wild, ringing cries echoing back
from the tall surrounding spruce forest. Anne had her own
log cabin which she had built in an even more remote spot
overlooking Black Bear Lake. She paddled us by canoe to
see beavers building their dams and to watch a big porcupine
climbing a tree.

Anne La Bastille is a girl who loves the wilderness. Her
little log cabin and her twenty-two acres of virgin forest,
miles from civilization, are her idea of heaven on earth.
There is no road to her cabin and when she is immured by
the deep snows of winter she tolerates her isolation, getting
about on snowshoes or snowmobile and drawing her water
from a hole cut in the lake ice. Although only five feet four
inches tall, she swings an axe like a miniature lumberjack
and is completely self-reliant. Yet in spite of her preference
for a spartan life, she remains essentially feminine and is by
no means a recluse.

Anne has made a distinguished name for herself as a
biologist and conservationist. At Cornell University she
obtained her Ph.D. in wildlife ecology in 1969 and held an
Assistant Professorship there. Previously she had been responsible for a number of important research projects concerned
with endangered species in the Caribbean and Central and
South America. It was, however, her work on the giant grebes
of Lake Atitlán from 1964 onwards which brought her to the
forefront among international conservationists.

The giant pied-billed grebe was not described for science
until 1929, though specimens of undetermined identity had
been collected in Lake Atitlán as early as 1862. The bird is
twice the size of the familiar 'hell-diver', as the Americans
call the pied-billed grebe of the United States. It has the
big-headed, tail-less appearance of the European grebes, but
with a prominent white eye-ring and a very heavy, black-
banded white bill. The plumage is blackish. Unlike other
grebes, however, it is flightless and unable to walk upright.
Its wings, though still of normal shape, have regressed in the

course of evolution to a size no longer able to support it in flight.

The geographical isolation of Lake Atitlán and the great depth of its water (1200 feet) have encouraged evolutionary changes, in the same way that they occur on isolated islands. All grebes dive for food, but in this lake the aquatic vegetation and food sources are at much greater depth than in other lakes. This led of necessity to the development of a more powerfully built bird, with an emphasis on deep-diving ability. Food was plentiful in the lake, the climate equable and predation by land animals avoided by an aquatic existence; therefore the grebe's migratory urge died out and the need for the ability to fly diminished. Although the volcanic lake was probably deficient in fish in its early stages, it is believed to have had a plentiful population of freshwater crabs. This, Anne believes, led to the evolution of the very massive bill and powerful jaw-muscles of the giant grebe, which became a specialized crab-eating diver, unique among the eighteen species of this family. Two of its closest relatives, the short-winged grebe of Lake Titicaca in Bolivia and the puna grebe of Lake Junin in Peru, also exist only in very high and isolated mountain lakes, but though also flightless these are much more 'normal' birds, both physiologically and in behaviour.

Lake Atitlán is in a steep-sided oval subsidence depression about thirteen miles long. It lies some fifty miles from Guatemala's Pacific coast, at an elevation of 5123 feet above sea level. There are several active volcanoes in the region. Until the 1960s it was a remote and unchanging habitat for wildlife. The Cakchiquel and Tzutuhil Indians in their little villages along the lake shores, descendants of the Mayas, depended chiefly on fishing for a livelihood. They did little harm to wildlife, killing only small numbers of waterfowl, including the giant grebes, with sling-shots. They were too poor for guns.

The Indians called the giant grebe the *poc*, an onomatopoeic interpretation of one of its call-notes. They had many strange beliefs about it. For example, they firmly believed that if a hunter was trying to shoot one, it would dive to the bottom of the lake, seize hold of some vegetation and hang on until it drowned. They confidently told Anne that it could stay submerged for half an hour and that it could swim beneath this surface for half a mile. Her careful studies disproved this: its maximum ability to stay submerged is about 100 seconds and the longest distance swum underwater at one breath about 300 feet.

Lake Atitlán and its surroundings are now changing rapidly. In 1958 and 1960 large-mouth bass were introduced to improve the sport-fishing, with disastrous consequences. These voracious and predatory fish, some of which grow to fifteen pounds in weight, not only soon ruined the native fishing industry, but preyed on young water-birds, including nestling giant grebes. The freshwater crabs, which the Indians harvested in large numbers, were driven by the bass to deeper waters where they could not be collected. To supplement the loss of protein, the Indians began taking more waterfowl, including grebes. Another problem, increasing yearly with the growing Indian population, was reed-cutting. This in turn meant a loss of breeding habitat for the grebes and increased disturbance to other aquatic life of the lake. Thoughtless introductions of alien species of fish, animals or plants almost invariably result in a chain-reaction of disasters such as these.

Following the introduction of the large-mouth bass, the heavy hand of 'developers' fell on Lake Atitlán. In quick succession a long series of plots of the lake shore were sold to wealthy Guatemalans and foreigners for the construction of holiday villas. With the occupants came the usual paraphernalia of holiday resorts such as water-skiing, scuba-diving, power-boating and, of course, hotels. The days of the giant pied-billed grebe seemed surely numbered when Anne started work there.

At the time of her arrival at Lake Atitlán, the giant grebe was one of the world's least-known birds. Practically nothing was known of its life history or behaviour. Its population was thought to be between 200 and 300 birds and nobody knew it was declining. As a result of Anne's first reports disproving these figures the species was listed in the IUCN *Red Date Book* of endangered birds with three stars, denoting that it was 'in grave danger'. Her task was to discover its exact status, the reasons for its decline and the measures which might be taken to ensure its survival. To do this, she had to know everything about the bird and its ecological requirements. The fact that her subject was exceptionally shy and spent much of its time underwater or hidden in the reed-beds, made her task a formidable one. No such work is easy even in favourable conditions. I would personally regard the study of animals in the African savanna from the comfort of a well-equipped Land-Rover infinitely more pleasant than having to spend hundreds of hours in a small open boat, facing the violent winds and sometimes storms for which Lake Atitlán is famous.

Anne's first important discovery, the result of several painstaking censuses, was that the population of grebes had dropped in five years from between 200 and 300 birds to only 80. If such a rate of loss continued, the species would certainly be extinct in another five years. Only a full-scale conservation effort with government backing could save it. Skill and determination she had in plenty, but the kind of conservation effort needed would involve the expenditure of a considerable amount of money. It seemed unlikely that the Guatemalan government, or any other government for that matter, could provide the necessary funds quickly enough to produce results in time. She remembered, however, that the World Wildlife Fund had been created to help in emergencies such as this and sent off a carefully documented appeal for help. Similar appeals were made to the Smithsonian Institution and the National Geographic Society. All three bodies were sufficiently impressed to respond positively. Grants were indeed made to enable her to continue her work for the following four years.

Armed with the assurance of financial support, Anne then approached the Guatemalan government. She had already drafted a comprehensive plan, which she showed to the

Minister of Agriculture and the Director of the Museum of
Natural History in Guatemala City. They were intrigued by
the eloquence and obvious expertise of this energetic young
gringa (Yankee girl), who had taken the trouble to learn
Spanish and was so enthusiastic about the poc. They liked
her proposed title for the plan, too. She had called it *Opera-
ción Protección del Poc*, which had a business-like tone. The fact
that big international foundations were backing her was also
impressive. They not only agreed to co-operate, but did so
with a will.

A full-time warden with a patrol boat was appointed to
guard Lake Atitlán and Anne was made an honorary
warden. Smart uniforms bearing the yellow and black badge
of the poc were provided. By presidential decrees, the reed
and cat-tail beds were put out of bounds to the reed-cutters
during the breeding season and the hunting of waterfowl
was banned. All the villages in the area of the lake were then
visited by Anne and the warden, and, with the help of the
Director of the Museum of Natural History, lectures and
explanations were given to the local mayors, villagers and
schoolchildren. The Indians are a taciturn people, who
hitherto had regarded wildlife only as an occasional source of
food. Anne had learned during her previous work on the
beautiful emerald-green and crimson quetzal (the national
bird of Guatemala) that Indians could readily be interested
in a bird which was important and honoured in Mayan
culture; but the poc was far from beautiful and had no
cultural background. Anne gave it a personality, explaining
that it was unique in the world and, therefore, a matter of
pride to all Guatemalans.

However, when one is very poor and uneducated, pride
in a national treasure is not easily engendered. Anne realized
this and wisely changed her approach. She pointed out that
the poc was attracting tourists to Lake Atitlán. If carefully
preserved, it would earn money for the villagers. They
should embody its image in their arts and crafts, she said,
and tourists would buy them. Gradually the idea was
accepted and the restrictions imposed by the presidential

decrees were obeyed. Tourists *did* buy the trinkets and rugs with the poc symbol.

Another spring came and Anne settled down again to begin her long study of the breeding behaviour of the grebes. It was an exacting task, but knowledge that she was the first person ever to attempt it spurred her on.

The courtship of the giant grebes is elaborate, as it is with all birds of this family. But whereas the courtship of our familiar great crested grebe is a beautiful aquatic ballet, that of the giant grebe is a mixture of the spectacular and the aggressive. To begin with, the establishment of nesting territories is accompanied by loud cries and fierce fighting. Any grebe trespasser near the chosen tract of reeds or cat-tails is instantly attacked. The defending male gives a first warning by aggressive posturing. This consists of a forward threat, in which it advances half-submerged with its head thrust out, its throat swollen and its neck kinked, like a snake about to strike. Often it rushes forward like a torpedo, creating a high bow-wave and then disappears in a powerful dive, its big lobed feet throwing up a fountain of water. The trespasser usually retreats in the face of this frightening spectacle. The defender then surfaces and works off its aggression by vigorous false-preening.

Another aggressive sequence, which Anne calls 'the bridling dog display', occurs when two males meet on a territorial boundary. Both pivot opposite each other, false-preening rapidly, then come face to face with heads and tails stiffly erect and throats distended to show the black throat-patches to advantage. Actual physical combat may take place on or beneath the water, the antagonists grappling breast to breast and slashing with their powerful bills in a flurry of flying spray. Chasing on the surface is often protracted.

In order to study this behaviour by males and paired birds more closely, Anne constructed and painted a scale model of a grebe, which she tethered near a breeding territory. To make it more life-like she played tape-recordings of the male territorial cries from her boat near by. She also experimented with the use of mirrors, so that defending males could attack their own reflections. After weeks of patient observation she was able to piece together the complete sequence of actions and their significance.

Having carefully mapped the breeding territories, the next step was to study nest building, egg laying, incubation and care of the nestlings. Finding the carefully hidden nests involved arduous searching in the almost impenetrable eighteen-foot-high reed-beds, growing in four feet of water. David Allen from Ithaca, New York, under the auspices of the *National Geographic*, joined her in some of this work and obtained a unique series of photographs of the parent grebes and their prettily striped puff-ball chicks, the first ever recorded. By the end of that year's work, the reproductive cycle of the giant grebes had been almost fully recorded. Even the behaviour of the birds below water had been studied by Anne, with the aid of scuba-diving equipment.

Anne was now able to identify quite clearly the factors on which the survival of the grebes depended. She summarized them as follows: they required a plentiful supply of small fish and crabs, plus aquatic insects and invertebrates which could be swallowed by both adults and young; a sufficient habitat of continuous and undisturbed reeds and cat-tails for roosting, nest building and breeding territories; a fairly stable water level, so that food sources remained accessible; relief from the predatory large-mouth bass; relief from human disturbance; finally, no volcanic or seismic activity to endanger the lake. (Active volcanoes were not far distant.) Her studies also enabled her to make an accurate assessment of the ultimate 'carrying capacity' of Lake Atitlán in the event of the grebe population increasing. It could sustain a maximum of only 280 birds, according to its size and resources of food. This last calculation and her worry about the large-mouth bass led her to visit all the other mountain lakes in Guatemala in the hope of finding a potential over-spill or alternative reserve, but none proved suitable. If the giant pied-billed grebe was to survive, it could only be at Lake Atitlán.

The widespread propaganda throughout Guatemala and elsewhere which 'Operation Poc' had created was meanwhile taking effect. The government had even issued a colourful set of postage stamps depicting Lake Atitlán, the poc and its fluffy chick, which were quickly sold out for a total of $123000. With the help of the World Wildlife Fund, an enclosed refuge of about three acres had been created in a small bay on the lake, where two captured pairs of pocs were released. The enclosure had plenty of reeds and cat-tails and the predatory bass had been removed from its open water. A small information centre was constructed beside the refuge and it proved instantly popular. Here tourists and local people could learn about the importance of the birds and could photograph them without causing disturbance to the wild population. A WWF signboard with the panda symbol now reminds Guatemalans of the world-wide interest in the famous poc.

Anne had achieved a great deal at Lake Atitlán. One of the remarkable aspects of her work was her demonstration that, with sympathy and understanding, it was possible to enlist the co-operation even of the withdrawn and 'difficult' Cakchiquel and Tzutuhil Indians, whose ancestral home was the shores of the lake. Despite their initial indifference, many of them ended by working with her and for her. She could feel proud when she learned that amongst themselves they called her 'Mama Poc'.

It was something of a tragedy when, just as everything seemed to be going so well, news came of a plan to build a huge hydroelectric installation on Lake Atitlán, to provide power for Guatemala City and the populated lowlands on the Pacific slope. It would be financed by the World Bank and the Guatemalan government and would cost $115m. Its effect on the lake and on the giant grebes would clearly be disastrous. The lake level would be drastically lowered and its crystal-clear waters badly polluted. The World Wildlife Fund and other conservation bodies were instantly alerted and representations were made at the highest levels to prevent such a catastrophe. At the time of writing, the scheme has been suspended while possible alternative sites are being examined. It is unthinkable that the Guatemalan government will willingly destroy a lake which many people describe as the most beautiful in the world, or that having recognized the poc as a national treasure they will allow it to be exterminated by the civil engineers.

Assuming this to be so, the future of the flightless giant pied-billed grebe seems secure. Thanks to Anne La Bastille's devoted work, its population had risen from a bare 80 in 1965 to 230 and it was being very carefully protected. For her outstanding contribution to conservation Anne was awarded the World Wildlife Fund Gold Medal in 1974 and it was richly deserved. At the presentation ceremony in Geneva, none of us was particularly surprised when this adventurous young woman hobbled forward to receive the medal from HRH Prince Bernhard, then President of the WWF, with her leg in plaster. She had recently broken her pelvis by falling from the roof of a truck, on which she had been standing to photograph some Canada geese, to illustrate an article she had written for the *National Geographic*!

7

THE ISLAND MEN FORGOT

OF all the tropical islands I have visited, and they are many, Aldabra is the strangest. My old friend Roger Tory Peterson, the doyen of American naturalists, called it 'a hostile paradise' and this is no bad description. Aldabra is anything but welcoming, yet once one is inside the reef it has a strange beauty and a fascination unlike that of any other island in the Indian Ocean.

It is wonderfully remote – 270 miles north-west of Malagasy and some 350 from the coast of Tanzania. There has never been any reason for ships to call there and it is far from any regular shipping lane. Landing on it can be dangerous and my first attempt was abortive.

Aldabra is an uplifted coral atoll, shaped like a hollow axe-head, with the blade towards the west. From east to west it is about twenty miles long and about eight at the widest part. But the atoll is really not much more than a narrow rim of dead coral surrounding a huge lagoon. Inside, the water is vivid green, outside, where the ocean floor drops away, is indigo blue. The whole is protected by a submerged and razor-sharp living coral reef. There are only four safe channels through it, one to the west and three on the north side. All are difficult to navigate, particularly on an ebbing tide, when the water boils through in a racing torrent; but they can be negotiated safely at high tide when conditions are favourable. They were far from ideal on my first attempt. A typhoon was reported somewhere in the south and the sea

D

was choppy, with a rising wind. We made it safely to the entrance of the main channel, where the surf was seething over the hidden coral, when a squall struck, bringing with it torrential rain. To continue would have been foolhardy, so our rubber Zodiac was put about and we headed back to the *Lindblad Explorer*, which was anchored about a mile away. Within a few minutes waves were breaking right over our little craft, so that we had to bale with our hats and anything else which would hold water. Zodiacs are virtually unsinkable, but in a high sea are like corks bouncing among the waves. Ours did everything but capsize. By the time we reached the sheltered side of the ship, the waves were twenty feet high and we had difficulty in leaping one by one to the pitching gangway.

On the second attempt conditions were perfect. As we passed the reef into the sheltered sixteen-mile-wide lagoon, it was like entering another world. The shallow emerald water was as transparent as glass, its surface barely ruffled by the wind. Tropical fish of every shape and colour glittered beneath us, among them occasional leisurely sharks, huge moray eels and rays as big as dining tables. On the dark green surrounding mangroves, hundreds of red-footed boobies, sacred ibises, frigatebirds, herons and egrets sat somnolently on their nests, eyeing us inscrutably. Above us wheeled graceful red-tailed tropicbirds, gleaming white fairy terns and thousands more frigates soaring on angular, seven-foot wings. Here and there, like giant toadstools, were wide circular tables of raised coral on narrow eroded stems, overhanging the water; these curious flat-topped islands formed convenient grandstands for resting and nesting seabirds. This was a strange, secret world of colour and movement, unimagined by those beyond the thunder of the protective reef.

But there was much more to Aldabra than the great lagoon. When we presently found a sheltered beach and landed, we discovered the animals for which the island has for centuries been known – the giant tortoises. A survey has shown that there are more than 80000 of them. After seeing the very small numbers surviving on the Galápagos Islands in the Pacific, it was astonishing to find the Indian Ocean race in such vast quantities. They lay in immobile groups of tens or twenties under every stunted tree, sheltering close-packed from the grilling sun. Among them, busily snapping up flies, were numerous little green geckos, which scuttled over and under the great domed carapaces like the parasite-hunting oxpecker birds on African buffaloes. Along the sand beach were the wide chevron tracks of the huge green turtles which land on Aldabra to lay their eggs. Red robber crabs nearly two feet wide waved their immense claws at me as I passed. The heat, radiated from the coral sand and rocks, was overpowering and I pitied the cold-blooded tortoises whose heavy shells were hot to the touch even in the deepest shade.

I walked inland beyond the narrow strip of coastal vege-tation and met a scene at once startling and repellent. In front of me stretched a great plain of jumbled, broken reef-rocks, like a chaotic white lunar landscape. In the middle distance a single giant tortoise, which must have weighed the best part of 300 pounds, was lurching and pitching with infinite slowness as it tried to cross the shimmering wilder-ness. It reminded me of a tank attempting to cross the con-crete 'dragon's teeth' of the Siegfried Line during the last war. As many of the crevasses in the coral appeared almost bottomless, I had a feeling that the poor beast would not make it, but half an hour later it was still persevering. I tried walking among the pinnacles and potholes, but it was like trying to cross a field of upturned bayonets which fractured at every step. I realized then why Peterson had called Aldabra 'a hostile paradise'. A broken ankle or death by thirst were all an explorer could expect in this part of the atoll.

Aldabra is unique in having escaped almost completely from interference by man and from the curse of introduced domestic animals. It is true that there are a few feral chickens and goats, but the scarcity of food, or perhaps disease, has prevented them from multiplying. As on most isolated islands, many of the land birds which arrived there as vagrants have gradually developed into new species or races. Among those to be found nowhere else is a large and very beautiful pigeon with dark blue plumage and a pale grey head, and a colourful little fody (a kind of weaver) which is scarlet and yellow. Aldabra has its own green and purple sunbird, a bulbul, a white-eye, a drongo, a brush warbler, a turtle dove and a coucal, all of them unique. Among the larger birds is a new race of flamingo and a little kestrel which nests in the coconut palms. Most interesting of all is a unique flightless rail, a delightfully inquisitive bird which eagerly comes forward when called by appropriate clicking noises. There are two small bats about which little is yet known and a large fruit bat which flies in daylight over the nesting colonies of boobies, like a big brown crow. Aldabra has many more insect species than any other atoll in the Indian Ocean and one-quarter of its butterflies and moths are found nowhere else.

Thirty miles south of the atoll lies Assumption Island, which, like the Mascarenes on the other side of Malagasy, provides a classic object lesson in human exploitation. It once had a unique population of endemic bird species and huge colonies of nesting seabirds. Today it is an almost lifeless, treeless desert island, its whole surface having been stripped away during the exploitation of its rich guano deposits. There was a short-term financial gain to the exploiters, but guano has now been superseded by chemical fertilizers. The extermination of the birds of Assumption was a tragedy which can never be justified. Fortunately there seemed no risk that Aldabra should ever be threatened with a similar fate as it has no guano worth taking and no apparent reason for man ever to interfere with it. Even the pirates who had terrorized shipping between East Africa and Europe had given it a wide berth and the few who had sought its shelter had usually left their bones on the reefs.

Aldabra was not even charted until 1878. Scientific expeditions to it were few. Charles Darwin called there in HMS *Beagle* and was sufficiently impressed to urge that its

unique fauna should be protected. When the government of
Mauritius later announced its intention to colonize the atoll,
Darwin's authority was respected and the plan was dropped.
Not until 1892 was a serious attempt made to collect specimens of the fauna and flora of Aldabra, by the American
scientist, Dr W. L. Abbott, after whom the rare Abbott's
booby was named. More information was obtained in 1905
by the Percy Sladen Trust expedition and in 1908 by
J. C. F. Fryer. Italian and American expeditions took place
in 1953 and 1954. Then came the much more important
work of the Bristol University expedition of 1964–65, which
provided the first detailed appreciation of Aldabra's treasures. Malcolm and Mary Penny, whom I had visited while
they were doing research in the Seychelles, produced with
Roger Gaymer an invaluable documentation during this
expedition. Finally, in 1966, came a visit of a very different
nature. It was organized not by naturalists but by the
British Ministry of Defence and the United States Air
Force.

The object of this expedition was to survey Aldabra in
preparation for converting it into a military air base and
radio station, for the control of the western reaches of the
Indian Ocean.

When news of this intention leaked out it aroused the
utmost consternation in scientific circles. Under the auspices
of the Royal Society, the world's most distinguished scientific
body, a conference was convened and it was decided to
attach Dr D. R. Stoddart of Cambridge University to the
proposed expedition, as the Society's representative. With
him went Dr Christopher Wright, representing the British
Museum (Natural History). Their instructions were to plan
an immediate programme of ecological research and to
recommend what measures of conservation might still be
possible in the light of the military threat to the atoll.

Dr Stoddart's report on his return was emphatic and well
documented. In effect it said that the construction of an airstrip and transmitter, with their attendant buildings, not
only entailed the virtually complete destruction of the atoll

and its wildlife, but, on such terrain, would represent an engineering task of gigantic and indeed idiotic proportions. The bulldozers would cause irreparable losses to science. Moreover, only thirty miles away there was a better and much easier site on the already ruined island of Assumption.

Another conference was held, this time attended by representatives from other senior scientific bodies such as the American Academy of Sciences and the International Council for Bird Preservation. The news had by now become public and indignant letters began to appear in the press. The general public, knowing nothing of Aldabra nor even where it was, nevertheless relished the notion of a battle between scientists and the government. When questions in the House of Commons elicited only vague and embarrassed replies from the ministers concerned, the press gave the Royal Society added support. Headlines such as 'The Flightless Rail versus the VC–10' began to appear.

While the controversy raged, a new figure came on the scene. Tony Beamish, a well-known explorer and maker of wildlife films, had been working in the Malayan jungle, where filming is particularly difficult. He longed for the sunlight and open skies of islands such as the Seychelles and was planning to visit them when he learned of the threat to Aldabra. Being a crusader at heart, the opportunity to contribute to the fight by making a film about Aldabra was irresistible. He hastened to London to consult everyone who knew anything about the atoll and its problems. Scarcely having heard of Aldabra before, he had very little idea of the difficulty of getting there, much less of filming the wildlife. He paid close attention, nevertheless, to one authority, who described the atoll as 'the most inhospitable place on earth' and equipped himself with suitable care. He then located a small Seychellois vessel, the 160-ton *Lady Esme*, which could take him from Mombasa to the atoll.

Tony Beamish was fortunate in his two companions on board. One was Guy Lionnet, Director of Agriculture and Fisheries of the Seychelles, who was also responsible for Aldabra, the other was Harold Hirth, a young professor

from the University of Utah and an expert on turtles. The
three were kindred spirits and widely experienced naturalists.

Their subsequent adventures on the atoll are vividly
described in Tony Beamish's book* and in the very fine
documentary film which he made. Both later became considerable assets in the battle to save Aldabra. When he and
his companions were landed at an old camp site called Anse
Mais their plan was simple and cheerfully optimistic – to
walk right round the rim of the atoll in ten days, filming and
photographing as they went. The circumference of the atoll
is, however, nearly seventy miles following its jagged contours; for most of the way two miles an hour would be fast
going even unencumbered by heavy equipment. The fact
that they succeeded in walking most of the way says much
for their resolution. The remainder was explored by boat
or by wading. Camps were made at five different sites. By
then their boots and feet were cut to shreds by the coral and
their faces mahogany-coloured by the sun. Radio communication with the absent *Lady Esme* was lost on the very
first day and was not regained.

They had been warned that if a typhoon approached they
would have to be rescued in a hurry; but they were undeterred by their total isolation and worked with unflagging
enthusiasm. All the wildlife was filmed, including the flamin-
goes, which very few people had previously seen. A flightless
rail even came into their tent at night to forage for food.
When the *Lady Esme*, which had been delayed by storms,
eventually appeared, they left the atoll with regret and a
passionate determination to do everything in their power to
prevent the threatened destruction of this extraordinary
little island paradise.

Tony Beamish is an excellent public speaker. I heard him
speak with missionary zeal on the subject of Aldabra at
several meetings. Unlike the typical scientist, who must be
carefully precise and unemotional, he used emotive words

*Beamish, Tony, *Aldabra Alone*, Allen & Unwin, London, 1970.

such as 'an international scandal' and the audience loved it. His film *Island in Danger* was magnificent and was seen by seven million people at its first showing on television. There is no doubt that it was a major factor in stimulating both the public and politicians to protest against the government's stubborn determination to proceed with the Anglo-American plans. People could now judge for themselves the fascination of the atoll's wildlife. Those of us engaged in the fight were overjoyed to have the film available.

The first indication that the views of the Royal Society and the growing resentment of the public were beginning to take effect came in a guarded statement by the Under Secretary of State for Air, who admitted that the government plan had 'caused concern in scientific circles'. He promised that scientific considerations would be taken into account. This first small crack in the armour of officialdom was carefully noted.

Dr Stoddart had meanwhile prepared a much more detailed document, setting out all the reasons why science and conservation attached so much importance to Aldabra. His memorandum was endorsed by the Natural Environment Research Council and others concerned and circulated to the Ministry of Defence. It was then followed up by a top-flight delegation from the Royal Society to meet Mr Denis Healey, at that time the Minister of Defence. It was headed by no less eminent a person than its distinguished President, Professor P. N. S. Blackett. The minister was told firmly that the Royal Society and all other British and American scientific institutions were unanimous in their conviction that 'any extensive development of Aldabra will inevitably destroy the greater part of those biological features – the result of a long period of evolution in isolation – which make it unique among the atolls of the world'.

Mr Healey was polite but unimpressed. There were compelling reasons, he said, why alternative sites could not be used. Nor could he encourage the delegation to hope that the government's plan would not be implemented.

Undeterred by the rebuff, the Royal Society sent a team

of eleven experts, led by Dr Stoddart, back to Aldabra to
conduct more detailed research which was to continue until
the spring of 1968. The establishment of so large a scientific
presence on the atoll might yet deter the bulldozers.

During this stalemate, public interest began to wane. As
the scientific aspects of the case appeared to make no impression on the government, the conservation bodies tried a
new approach, this time concentrating on the immense
practical difficulties of turning the atoll into a military air-
base, to overcome which the public would have to pay an
extortionate price. A letter was sent to *The Times*, signed by
Peter Scott, representing the World Wildlife Fund, Professor
W. H. Thorpe, on behalf of the Royal Society, the Marquess
of Willingdon, representing the Fauna Preservation Society,
and Tony's cousin, Sir Tufton Beamish, our chief ally in the
House of Commons. The main argument put forward is
worth quoting:

The island has no harbour and is composed of coral rock, under-
mined and dissected by the sea. The plan is to dam the lagoon,
which is tidal and the size of the Thames estuary, to make a port
and then to build a causeway twenty miles long. Even before the
construction is complete, the scientific value of the island will have
been irreversibly damaged. Then the authorities will have to
overcome the problem of bird–aircraft collisions – likely at
Aldabra to be the worst in the world . . . It appears incredible
folly to embark on such a project without a proper on-the-site
survey and costing of the various other islands in the area to
which there is no scientific objection and where the frigatebird
problem does not arise. The whole project, besides involving
enormous and unstated expense, appears extremely hazardous.

This hit the government where it was most vulnerable,
for no proper survey of alternative sites had been made and
no estimate of cost had appeared. Immediately, a fresh and
stimulating correspondence from many distinguished people
followed in *The Times*. Sir Julian Huxley added his presti-
gious name to the cause in a powerfully argued letter. Dr
Bill Bourne, a leading authority on seabirds, demolished the
RAF view that the bird-strike problem could be overcome,

by pointing out that the American Air Force had not yet overcome it after killing thousands of albatrosses which nested on their airfield on Midway Island. On Aldabra there were more than a million frigatebirds alone!

The RAF Air Marshals loyally supported their minister in print, but by trying to minimize the harm the project would do, only invited better-informed rebuttals. It was useless for someone who had not visited Aldabra to write that 'only an extremely small proportion of the island would be affected', when half a dozen well-qualified people who knew the atoll were ready to quote facts which made nonsense of the RAF view.

A particularly good summary of the conservationist attitude appeared in the authoritative *New Scientist*: 'The Union Jack flying over Aldabra is evidence of our custodianship of a biological treasure house. It is not a licence to kill.' On the other side of the Atlantic the National Academy of Sciences of the United States made sure there was no wavering of American public opinion, by emphasizing that 'The Academy and the Royal Society have urged their governments to exert every effort to eliminate this threat of incalculable damage to one of the world's unique resources for scientific investigation.' The influential Smithsonian Institution and the National Wildlife Federation joined in with urgent pleas that American participation in the Aldabra scandal should cease. Reassurance to this effect was finally given by the US Secretary for Defence, Robert S. McNamara (himself a conservation-conscious politician). In reply, he wrote: 'The importance of Aldabra as a scientific laboratory is fully recognized throughout our government. We have notified officialy the concern of the US scientific community to the British.' The fear that a change of heart might offend our American allies was thus removed and the decision became entirely a British responsibility.

The debate now raged chiefly in the House of Commons. More than a hundred embarrassing questions were raised by various members, though the Speaker did his best to have the subject dropped. Tony Beamish's television film and several very outspoken debates which it inspired egged on the protectionists.

Suddenly the whole thing collapsed. Not by any magnanimous intention of the government, but because the pound was devalued. In the briefest possible terms, the Prime Minister announced that for economic reasons the Aldabra plan had been dropped. There were celebrations in the conservation camp, but they were short-lived. Challenged to make the position absolutely clear, the Minister of Defence admitted that the conversion of Aldabra into a strategic Air Force staging post had not been cancelled, but postponed. Future British or American governments might ultimately still decide to implement the plan, he said.

Nevertheless, as things turned out, Aldabra is now secure. It is now no longer part of the British Indian Ocean Territories, but part of an independent Seychelles Republic. The Royal Society had a lease which enabled it to build a small research station and laboratory equipped with solar distillation, by the West Channel, for the young scientists working on the island. The government's plan was in any event very unlikely ever to have been implemented after the decision to withdraw our now very limited military resources to Europe. Nor were the United States ever likely to re-open the subject. By calling it a postponement, the British government was merely saving face, which in view of its embarrassment was perhaps understandable. As Dr Leach said in his Reith Lecture that year: 'Devaluation has at least prevented you from aiding and abetting an international crime.'

The importance of the Aldabra story lies in the fact that a decision taken by politicians for a temporary military advantage was successfully challenged by scientists. The august Royal Society, to whom the main credit is due, had never before meddled in politics. A noteworthy precedent had been set. Another advantage was that the very wide publicity given to the affair on both sides of the Atlantic aroused the public to the need for closer vigilance over government decisions taken without full disclosure of the likely consequences. Had the Royal Society not learned by chance of the plan, nor acted very quickly to assess the consequences, the public would not have heard of Aldabra until it was too late to protest.

Aldabra and its unique wildlife will now survive, as a living laboratory for science and as a place of wonder and delight to those fortunate people who may visit it. Moreover, this small island which men forgot is now recognized throughout the world at its true value. Plans are in hand to create an international foundation to assure its future protection, as was done for the Galápagos Islands.

8

THE HAWAIIAN RESCUE

THE Hawaiian archipelago in the middle of the Pacific has the dubious distinction of having lost fourteen of its native birds in the past two hundred years – a larger number than any other large island group in the world. Moreover, no fewer than twenty-nine of its surviving species are today listed as endangered.

The original Hawaiians, who came from Polynesia in the sixth century AD, undoubtedly killed many birds, notably the very colourful little honeycreepers of various kinds whose feathers were used for making their magnificent royal feather robes. But there is no evidence that they ever endangered the survival of any species. They were a quiet and contented people, whose culture reflected the beauty of their surroundings. As usual, it was the coming of the white man which heralded the extermination of wildlife. Captain Cook discovered the archipelago in 1778 and by the latter part of the nineteenth century the destruction of forests to make way for westernized agriculture had resulted in the first losses. The rapid spread of introduced dogs, cats, donkeys, pigs, goats, rats and other alien mammals (including the mongoose to kill the rats), as well as numerous alien birds and plants which carried with them diseases hitherto unknown on the islands, accelerated the process. One by one the unique birds of Hawaii began to disappear. Of the original twenty-two different honeycreepers, eight are now extinct and at least eight more nearing extinction. Part of the reason for their disappearance has been the replacement of the nectar-bearing flowers on which they depend by the spread of thoughtlessly introduced foreign plants. Competition with the introduced Japanese white-eye, a pretty but invasive little bird, has been another factor.

It is difficult today to imagine what the islands looked like when Captain Cook first saw them. We know that he was impressed by their beauty. But on the island of Oahu the famous holiday resorts such as Waikiki Beach are today almost indistinguishable from other American resorts; metropolitan Honolulu is a typical bustling American city and Pearl Harbour like any other great American naval base. Since their annexation by the United States in 1898, the main islands have in fact conformed to 'the American way of life' almost completely. Only on the remote little island of Niihau is the old Hawaiian language still spoken by every-one and all western devices such as telephones, automobiles, juke boxes and drugstores excluded. Pure-blood Hawaiians now represent little more than 2 per cent of the population of 600000. The original native dances, music and costumes have been largely replaced by bogus Hollywood-inspired imitations which, with the aid of electronics, spotlights and plastic materials, are more pleasing to the millions of tourists who make Hawaii prosperous. The pretty girls who entertain tourists on the dance floors of the skyscraper hotels are of mixed Polynesian, Japanese, Filipino, Chinese and Caucasian ancestry and few of them know the deep tradi-tional significance of the dances they mime so engagingly. Everything in the fiftieth state of the Union is now splendidly efficient and hygienic, but, at least to me, depressingly mass-produced and artificial. No nation has greater skill in con-servation in its widest sense than the United States, nor spends more on it and on the arts also. Yet, in its well-meaning desire to bestow the benefits of American civiliza-tion on its foreign possessions, it sometimes inflicts cultural losses which can never be restored.

Once one leaves the tourist cities of Hawaii behind, something of the original beauty of the islands can still be seen in the national parks and along the scenic driveways. But even here much has changed. Hundreds of species of trees and shrubs from other countries have been introduced. The effect is often beautiful, but it is not as Nature intended. The islands would have been a botanical paradise with their original 900 species of flowering plants and 140 species of graceful ferns, even without man's intervention. Perhaps more so, because many of the introductions are chronically invasive, smothering the native species and eventually replacing them.

Only when one climbs beyond the neatly terraced plantations of pineapple and sugar cane into the high tropical rainforest among the mountains and canyons, can an impression of the original scene be gained. Above the forest tower the great volcanic peaks, the highest of which, Mauna Kea on the island of Hawaii, reaches 13 784 feet. It is one of the highest island mountains in the world. Volcanic eruptions, earthquakes and giant tidal waves still occur in the archipelago and many of the islands have changed their contours and coastline since the days of Captain Cook.

Twenty-six miles north-west of Hawaii lies Maui, which, from a high-flying aircraft, looks exactly like the shape of a woman's head and bust. On the head and breast are two extinct volcanic peaks, joined by a low isthmus forming the six-mile-wide neck. The larger mountain, called Haleakala, 'The House of the Sun', rises more than 10 000 feet and has a crater twenty miles wide. The slopes of both mountains abound with magnificent canyons and on the windward side of Haleakala the forest shelters many spectacular waterfalls. It is on this beautiful island and on Hawaii itself that a remarkable effort to save a unique bird from extinction has now been crowned with success. The species concerned is the néné goose – now the state national bird.

Although goose enthusiasts would probably disagree with me, I regard some species of this numerous family as lacking in charm. Their movements on land are ponderous and their voices brazen. But no such criticism can be applied to the néné. It is an aristocrat among geese, refined in colouration and elegant in form and movement. It is small, a mere twenty-five inches from bill to tail. Its face and crown are black, as are its legs and its only partly webbed feet. Its neck is the colour of fresh cream, diagonally striped with black lines, the curiously pointed feathers being quite unlike those of its relatives the brent and barnacle geese. Its back and flanks are handsomely scalloped with dark brown and white crescentic markings. When it speaks, it does so with refined restraint, neither braying nor honking in the vulgar manner of many other geese. Even its way of life is distinguished, for it prefers to live in the solitude of high volcanic craters. It lays only three to five eggs, nesting at from 2000 to 5000 feet above sea level among old lava flows. From every point of view the néné is exclusive, a little Beau Brummel among geese.

It is believed that before Captain Cook's arrival the nénés had a fairly large population and that they may have occurred even down to sea level on Hawaii and perhaps also on Maui. The Polynesians used to hunt them when they retired to moult (when they became flightless) and to breed in the craters of Mauna Loa, Mauna Kea and other secluded places. They were, however, never endangered until the advent of firearms and feral domestic animals which destroyed their eggs and young and the vegetation on which they depended for food and nest sites. Their population is thought to have numbered about 25000 until that time, but by 1800 it had declined sharply. By 1900 it was restricted to a mere scattering of birds in the mountains of Hawaii only. Within the next decade the species would almost certainly have disappeared had it not been for two fortunate attempts at captive breeding.

The first attempt was made by Lord Derby in 1823 at Knowsley Park, Lancashire, where he had a private collection of ornamental fowl. He succeeded in rearing a sufficient number of nénés to supply several other collections. In 1832 Lady Glengall presented a pair from these offspring to the London Zoo, where Nicholas Vigors, Secretary of the Zoological Society of London, gave the species the scientific

There were fewer than thirty néné geese surviving in the world
when Sir Peter Scott began his successful captive-breeding
programme at the Wildfowl Trust.

Today nearly 2000 nénés are again thriving on the islands of
Hawaii and Maui, thanks to the Wildfowl Trust and the US
Department of Fish and Wildlife.

The world population of Asiatic lions had dropped to 177 when I visited their last refuge in the Indian Gir Reserve. Thanks to careful management the number now exceeds 200.

In spite of disturbance from a new airstrip and tourist lodge, a million sooty terns still nest on the half-mile-long Bird Island in the Indian Ocean.

The snow-white fairy terns build no nests but lay their single eggs in the oddest and most precarious places all over Cousin Island Reserve.

Right: La Digue Island in the Seychelles is famous for its unique paradise flycatchers, of which there are only about seventy pairs. The long-tailed male is black.

name *Anser sandvicensis*, after Lord Sandwich, whose name
the Hawaiian Islands had once borne. For many years the
zoo birds bred successfully and spread to other collections.
Lacking an intake of fresh blood, however, breeding success
soon declined and by 1912 very few were left. A male
reared in Holland in 1898 was the last survivor. Transferred
to Jean Delacour's collection at the Château de Clères in
France, it fell a victim to the German invasion in 1940, with
the distinction of having been the longest-lived goose ever
documented. I happened to be one of the first to see what
remained of Clères when I was with the British army of
liberation. Jean Delacour had been a friend of mine when I
had lived in France. He had escaped to New York, where I
later gave him my photographs of what had once been the
finest avicultural park in Europe.

In 1918, by which date it was obvious that the néné, both
as a wild species and in captivity, was near to extinction, a
new effort was made, this time in Hawaii. Harold C.
Shipman, a landowner and an experienced aviculturist,
began to breed captive nénés at Keeau. In 1927 the
Hawaiian Board of Agriculture and Forestry began a similar
venture. Both did well, each raising about forty birds. In
1935, however, the effort by the Board of Agriculture was
abandoned and in 1946 a great tidal wave struck Hawaii,
destroying most of Shipman's birds, though a few escaped
to the wild. By 1947 it was known that there were no captive
nénés left in Europe and no more than fifty – captive or wild
– in Hawaii. By 1951 the authorities in Hawaii reported the
total to be only thirty known birds. The species was again
tottering on the very brink of extinction.

The fate of the néné had for some while been a major
preoccupation to Peter Scott, then, as now, Chairman of the
Survival Service Commission of the IUCN and already the
leading expert on the world's wildfowl. The famous son of a
famous father, Scott of the Antarctic, Peter's career has been
one of astonishing virtuosity. He has earned renown as an
artist, a writer, a broadcaster, a distinguished naval officer
with a D.S.C. and bar, a gliding champion, an Olympic

medallist in yachting, a rector of one university and chancellor of another, and the founder of the Wildfowl Trust at Slimbridge, Gloucestershire. In 1970 he was knighted for his services 'to conservation and the environment' and it is in this sphere, as Chairman and one of the founders of the World Wildlife Fund, that his greatest contribution has been made. Wildfowl had been his dominant interest from an early age and it was natural that he should regard the survival of the néné goose as a personal challenge.

In 1950 Peter Scott sent John Yealland, at that time Curator of the Wildfowl Trust, to Hawaii. The Hawaiian Board of Agriculture still had two surviving pairs of Shipman's nénés, plus a gander from the Honolulu Zoo and a wild bird caught in 1949. These were assembled at a new game farm at Pohakuloa for a final attempt at captive breeding. It was decided that John Yealland should fly one pair back to Slimbridge, where these would be given the maximum skilled attention. There was some consternation, however, when both of them presently laid eggs and it was realized how difficult it was to distinguish the sexes in the néné. The Hawaiian Board of Agriculture generously agreed to send a known gander from their tiny flock of surviving birds and it reached Slimbridge safely. It was named Kamehameha, after the great Hawaiian king whose statue stands outside the Judiciary Building in Honolulu.

This noble bird and his two wives, named after two Hawaiian queens, Kaiulani and Emma, produced nine healthy goslings the following year. By the time of his death in 1963, Kamehameha had become the progenitor of no fewer than 230 néné geese, many of which were transferred to collections in other European countries and the United States as a precaution against the many diseases to which captive birds are subject. The avicultural standards at the Wildfowl Trust are probably the highest to be found anywhere. Its collection is unique, numbering as it does living examples of almost all the world's swans, geese and ducks. Moreover, thousands of wildfowl from Iceland, Greenland and northern Europe regularly visit the area around the

Trust grounds to feed during the migratory season. Some of them and particularly the wild swans, mingle with the captive birds on the ornamental pool outside Sir Peter Scott's big picture window.

Back in Hawaii the Pohakuloa breeding stock was also beginning to thrive under expert care. Much had now been learned about the requirements of these precious birds, which American biologists were studying in the wild. Legal protection for the néné had been given around 1910, though predation by the introduced mongoose and other feral pests continued to be a problem to the wild nesting birds. But public opinion was now strongly in favour of the beautiful little goose and its chances of survival steadily improved. As the captive stocks at Slimbridge and Pohakuloa increased, it was decided to begin experiments in returning some to the wild.

From 1962 to 1967 a total of 197 birds from the Wildfowl Trust were carried up the lava slopes of Maui and released. They appeared to settle in their traditional habitat contentedly. Even larger numbers were successfully returned to the wild on Maui and on Hawaii from the Pohakuloa breeding stock.

Four protected reserves were now available to the wild nénés and the US Congress had voted a substantial budget for continuing the breeding venture in Hawaii and for ecological research. By 1977 the total population of nénés in the wild had risen to nearly 2000 birds, with some 1250 from the Wildfowl Trust stock in various zoos and private collections. Bearing in mind that the world population, captive or wild, had fallen to only thirty birds by 1951, it was a magnificent achievement. The main credit goes to the very high skills shown by the Wildfowl Trust and the Pohakuloa game farm in overcoming the problems of raising a healthy and genetically viable population from such an extremely small original stock of captives.

At Slimbridge, the people chiefly concerned were Tommy Johnstone, Mike Lubbock and Dr Janet Kear, the Trust's Avicultural Co-ordinator; one of the Trust members, Jack

Williams, who also specialized in breeding nénés, contributed fifty of the birds which were returned to Maui, while Terry Jones, the Curator of the Leckford Waterfowl Collection, raised substantial further numbers. As with the Arabian oryx, zoos and private collectors had made a major contribution to conservation. Their efforts to save the néné had persisted, on and off, for more than a hundred and fifty years.

9

THE GARDEN OF INDIA

ALTHOUGH the state of Gujarat has been called 'the garden of India', it is not often included in the itinerary of the tourists who congregate in thousands to admire the palaces of Jaipur in the neighbouring state of Rajasthan. Nevertheless, though off the tourist beat, Gujarat is a beautiful part of the sub-continent and it has a fascinating history. Moreover, it can boast among its treasures the world's only surviving population of Asiatic lions. To see these magnificent creatures roaming beneath the flowering flame-of-the-forest trees in the Gir Forest is alone worth the rather tiresome journey from Bombay. One takes the somewhat erratic daily flight to Keshod and then continues by road for fifty-six miles to the Gir.

Gujarat occupies the blunt Kathiawar Peninsula, between the Gulf of Kutch and the Gulf of Cambay and the adjoining mainland north of Bombay. The fierce Muslim Gujars, who poured into India from the mountains in the far north-west in AD 400–600, have now been largely absorbed in this state by Hinduism, which today represents 80 per cent of the population. The British, with an eye to the strategic value of Junagadh's access to the Indian Ocean, made a friendly accommodation with the ruler in 1807, giving him a suitably high ranking in the always delicate protocol concerning the number of gun-salutes to which he would be entitled on ceremonial occasions. The last ruler, His Highness Sir Mahabat Khan Babi Pathan, Nawab of Junagadh, was, like most of the great Indian princes, a picturesque figure who delighted in splendour.

He was also an eccentric. At one time he was the proud owner of 800 pedigree dogs of various breeds, each with its own room, electric light and uniformed servant. According to John Lord,* the cost of upkeep of this astonishing canine establishment was £32 000 a year. This sum, however, excluded the cost of the elaborate state weddings and funerals of the Nawab's favourite dogs, which were conducted with lavish pomp and ceremony, involving bejewelled dog-garments and processions of painted and gilded elephants.

As the inevitability of Partition drew nearer, there was much anxiety about the future of Junagadh and its picturesque ruler who, as a good Muslim, was an obvious candidate to join Pakistan. John Lord has described how the astute Indian government hastily dispatched a few squadrons of aircraft to fly over the Nawab's palace and circulated rumours that artillery and infantry were assembling on his frontiers. Regretfully, he decided that although his colourfully uniformed private army would probably fight bravely, it was unlikely to be able to stand up to modern artillery; so he fled quietly to a peaceful retirement in Pakistan. His abandoned population, not surprisingly since they were nearly all Hindus, speedily voted to become Indian citizens. Today, with the state having become a normal administrative district and part of Gujarat, the people scarcely remember their flamboyantly eccentric former ruler.

Though many of the hereditary princes of India were despotic and some frankly villainous in their treatment of enemies or potential competitors, almost all of those who survived Partition were cultured men and delightful hosts. One can appreciate how they must have felt to see their great palaces turned into tourist hotels, or left as empty, echoing monuments to an age of unlimited extravagance. Some of those who had sufficient funds abroad now wander disconsolately around the more opulent resorts of Europe; others

*Lord, John, *The Maharajahs*, Hutchinson, London, 1972.

have accepted the new régime and now hold ministerial positions in the states they once ruled, or are in the central government, where a few have risen by sheer ability to the highest levels. But with the passing of the maharajahs, good or bad, India has lost some of its heady glamour and will never be quite the same again.

Although I have visited India frequently, it was not until 1969 that I had occasion to spend a few days in Gujarat, where I made my way in a bouncing jeep to the tourist bungalow at Sasan, in the Gir Forest. It was at that time a depressing building, much in need of repair and used only by day trippers from the neighbouring towns. The air was heavy with the reek of disinfectant and the acrid smell of spices and burning cow dung. Hot and dusty, I sat on the verandah swatting flies while I waited for a drink. When it arrived it was tepid and already fringed with flies. A long string of zebu cattle and water buffaloes trudged slowly past, driven by a tiny *maldhari* girl of six or seven, who smiled shyly up at me. The dense cloud of dust they created settled like a pall around me, coating my drink with a yellow skin. Fortunately, the superintendent then arrived and triumphantly produced cold Coca Cola, which we drank while he told me about the Gir lions. I would have to wait until evening to see them, he said, because they would then be given a tethered young buffalo at the roadside.

'It's the only way to attract tourists,' he explained. 'You can't expect them to go looking for lions in the forest.'

It was to this, in fact, that the famous Gir reserve had been reduced. I had already read the well-documented report about it, written by Dr Paul Joslin of Aberdeen University, which we had debated at an international meeting of conservationists in New Delhi. It was a tragic story.

The Asiatic lion *Panthera leo persica* is a now isolated forest-dwelling race of the species which once occurred throughout the Old World. By AD 100 lions had disappeared from Europe and by the close of the nineteenth century were nearing extinction in the Middle East and North and South Africa. By 1908 probably no more than fifty survived in

Asia, all of them being in the Gir Forest. The creation of wildlife reserves in central Africa assured the survival of the lions in that continent, while in India the protection given by the Nawab of Junagadh to the Gir saved the Asiatic race literally at the last minute. He was proud of his lions and would only rarely permit a visiting VIP to shoot one. Their numbers gradually recovered and this was confirmed by a census made by the Indian Board for Wildlife in 1956. By 1963 the population had risen to 285 and in 1966, when a decline had become apparent, the government of Gujarat set aside 500 square miles of the forest as a 'lion sanctuary'. But at the time of my visit in 1969 the decline had again become catastrophic and only 177 remained. A simple calculation suggested that at such a rate of decline the population could drop to zero within twenty years.

The original Gir Forest covered an area exceeding one thousand square miles. It was teeming with game of all kinds and rarely disturbed except for occasional hunting by the ruler and his guests. After Partition, deterioration was immediate. In the scramble for possession of the Nawab's former property, the Gir was deeply eroded by villages and the spread of cultivation. Thousands of acres of forest were felled before the enthusiastic villagers could be brought under even partial control. Today very little of Gujarat is forested and the desert is advancing from the east into the 'garden of India'. Once a major watershed, the state is becoming short of water.

On paper, 500 square miles for only 177 lions looked fairly reasonable, but the reality was very different. The scarcity of grazing outside the reserve had resulted in a constant penetration of the forest by at least 21000 domestic cattle; during the monsoon the figure exceeded 50000. In consequence, the wild deer and antelope prey-species of the lions, such as the nilgai, sambur, chital, four-horned antelope and chinkara gazelle, had insufficient food and were disappearing. Most of the fertile valleys in the forest where they fed were occupied by settlers and the reserve had been cut to ribbons by cultivation. No fewer than 129 *nesses* (villages), peopled by nearly 5000 *maldharis* already existed within its boundaries. Few large trees remained and natural regeneration was minimal because of the intensive pressure of grazing by cattle. Moreover, the industrious *maldharis* were cutting and removing two million kilograms of fodder each year from the forest.

The biological potential of the reserve had become negligible and the lions were obliged to feed almost exclusively on domestic cattle. But even then they were seldom permitted to have a square meal. No sooner did they kill a cow or a water buffalo than they were driven off by the watchful *harijans*, the 'untouchables', whom Mahatma Gandhi had called 'the children of God'; their role in life includes the disposal of the meat, bones and hides of dead animals. Paul Joslin's studies showed that a quarter of all the cattle killed by lions were not eaten at all by them and that from another 20 per cent they were unable to take more than 10 kilogrammes of meat before being driven off by *harijans*. In order to retain the value of the lions as a tourist attraction, about 20 per cent of them were now regularly fed with tethered buffaloes. The remainder suffered from malnutrition. The birth-rate of the population had dropped to less than half that of the African lion, most of the cubs dying in the foetal stage or soon after birth.

It was a depressing situation and I set off that evening with little hope that I could do anything about it. I was accompanied by 'Ranjit' Ranjitsinh, who in the old days was entitled to be addressed as His Highness the Maharajkunar of Wankaner, a state north of Junagadh. 'Ranjit' was now a senior civil servant, but was greatly admired by all visiting experts from other countries for his extensive knowledge of Indian animals. He knew only too well the problems in the Gir.

After driving for only twenty minutes we saw the first lion and shortly afterwards several more. Against the urgent warnings of the guard in the back seat, I got out and walked slowly towards an adult male, which was resting in a teak plantation. It looked larger than most African lions. When it lifted its head and gave me a challenging look, I stopped. Reassured that I meant no harm, it yawned cavernously and rolled over on its back, paws in the air, in the attitude so often seen among African lions when they are lazing. I took some photographs at about sixty feet and returned to the car. The guard, who obviously did not care for lions, said 'It is not good', but I have photographed a dozing tiger with equal safety.

We drove on to where some chattering Indian tourists were standing by their bus. A hundred yards away a young buffalo stood dejectedly tethered to a tree. Twenty yards farther on a young male lion, a lioness and a half-grown cub lay among the trees watching it. After a while they rose and walked slowly towards the now terrified captive, which was straining at the rope. Without hurrying, the lioness toppled it over and broke its neck with a crunching bite behind the head; then began tearing mouthfuls of flesh from the still flailing back legs. The male and cub tried to join in, but were driven back with a bloody snarl. It was a degrading, man-made spectacle, but the tourists who had each paid ten rupees for it appeared satisfied, judging by their admiring cries. Our headlights later picked out several more lions at the roadside as we drove back to the bungalow.

'Well,' said Ranjit, 'you can see now why we can't expect to compete with the African game reserves.'

A few days later I discussed the Gir situation with my old friend Zafar Futehally, then Honorary Secretary and now Vice President of the World Wildlife Fund in India. Like Ranjit, he felt that bold and positive action must be taken.

'Unless we can break through the bureaucratic objections which block every move towards solutions, we shall be too late,' he said. 'The problems are now known to everyone and the Gujarat ministers *want* action to be taken. But saving the Gir lions is more than a local matter – it is a *national* responsibility. We need help from the highest possible level.'

'You mean Indira Gandhi?'

'Yes. If you send your report and recommendations on

behalf of the World Wildlife Fund international headquarters to the Governor of Gujarat *and* to the Prime
Minister it might do the trick.'

When I reached home I sat down with all the various
reports on the Gir written by the Indian Board for Wildlife
and visiting scientists such as Paul Joslin, Stephen Berwick,
George Schaller and Lee Talbot, from which I summarized
the problems and the evidence. Then I drafted the recommendations which they and I felt were essential if India's
national animal, 'the lion of Ashoka', was to be saved.
(Emperor Ashoka was the world's first conservationist. In
242 BC his fifth pillar edict gave protection to all wild
animals and plants; it was ironical that fourteen of his edicts
could still be seen chiselled on a huge granite boulder near
the Gir Forest.)

My recommendations called for a ten-year plan to restore
the Gir reserve to something like its former condition. The
first requirement was to re-settle all the *maldharis* and their
cattle outside the reserve, compensation for loss of land or
income being paid by the state. Second, a totally protected
inner sanctum should be created in the best part of the surviving forest, within which no disturbances of any kind should
be permitted. An all-weather jeep track should be constructed
around it for a daily patrol by guards. Third, the population
of deer and antelope should be increased in the inner sanctum, if necessary by translocation from other reserves; but
until numbers reached a satisfactory level to provide sufficient food for the lions, a limited number of domestic cattle
should be permitted to graze in the remainder of the reserve
and compensation should be paid for those taken by lions.
No carcasses should be taken by *harijans*. Fourth, all cultivated areas in the reserve should be sown with native
grasses, in order to provide food for the deer and antelope.
Probably five years would be required for this first stage.

The second half of the plan would involve the restoration
of the rest of the reserve, by the progressive withdrawal of
the remaining cattle. The deforested areas would be re-
planted with native trees, leaving areas of grazing in the

valleys. Once the lions had returned to catching their
restored wild prey, the practice of giving them tethered
domestic buffaloes, either to supplement their diet or as a
tourist attraction, would be prohibited. Finally, when fully
restored, the reserve should be given national park status
and could then earn substantial revenue under a carefully
managed plan for tourism in the perimeter areas. The
World Wildlife Fund and the Smithsonian Institution had
promised help in creating a wildlife research centre in the
reserve, at which local personnel could be trained as eco-
logists, park managers and guards. I concluded with a
reminder that all the experts, both Indian and foreign, were
unanimous in believing that unless action along these lines
could be taken quickly, there was little hope of saving the
lions. Zafar Futehally was pleased with the document and it
was dispatched to Mrs Gandhi and the Gujarat government.
I then went to the Galápagos Islands, on the other side of
the world, and was occupied with different conservation
problems.

When next I heard from Zafar the news was good. An
illustrated book entitled *The Gir Lion Sanctuary Project* had
been published by the Gujarat government, with an excellent
foreword by Shriman Narayan, the Governor of the state.
My proposals were included and had been adopted. Also
included were the texts of several government resolutions
concerning their implementation and details of a covering
budget of forty-five lakhs of rupees (£300000) for the first
five years. Ranjitsinh and the Indian Board for Wildlife had
obviously played an active part in helping to draft the
necessary legislation, which appeared to be admirable in
content. The re-settlement of the *maldharis* was fraught with
difficult social and political problems, but the Governor had
shown great courage in facing this issue, on which everything
else depended. Having seen the skill and humanity with
which a similar problem of translocation had been handled
in the Kanha tiger reserve in Madhyar Pradesh, I was
confident that he would succeed.

Nevertheless I had deep sympathy for the poor *maldharis*,

even though I knew they would be exchanging broken-down mud-built shacks in badly polluted villages for newly built homes on an unspoilt site. I knew also that, once restored, the new national park would bring increased employment to the community. But would they understand? I longed for the ability to break through India's impregnable barrier of fourteen languages and 280 local dialects, in order to be able to explain that the survival of representative areas of wilderness and wildlife was not the mere whim of a foreigner, nor merely to please officials or the rich, but something to benefit all mankind, including the *maldharis'* own children.

One stands before a desperately poor, blank-faced villager in the wilds of India, or the Congo, or the Amazon basin, it scarcely matters where in the Third World, faced with this inevitable problem of communication, which to me has become a cliché of appalling proportions. Even if one has managed to learn the rudiments of the principal language of the country, it is seldom spoken in the remote villages. Moreover, most native interpreters are barely literate and delight in turning the white man's carefully worded explanation of the need for certain actions to be taken into peremptorily bawled instructions. Will the villagers ever really understand why their hungry but destructive cattle must be excluded from a certain area, or why a certain wild animal must no longer be hunted?

There was always a risk, in India as elsewhere, that efforts to prevent the extinction of wildlife would be construed as putting the interests of animals before human needs. I myself had been attacked in the Indian press by a politically motivated writer, who declared that instead of trying to save the few surviving tigers I should be advocating their extermination, because they killed the cattle of poor villagers. There were, of course, also protests of a more obvious motivation, such as those from *shikar* companies, whose livelihood depended on selling equipment and organizing hunts for wealthy foreigners. One had to understand such protests. But the problem was deeper. Foreigners who presumed to tell Indians what was good for them, and sometimes even those who exercised the utmost diplomacy in genuinely trying to help Indians, had to learn the hard way that, since Mrs Gandhi had said 'India must stand on its own feet', there was a new spirit of nationalism which bred acute sensitivity towards foreign assistance or advice of any kind. Indeed many fervent Indian nationalists regard aid from other countries as abhorrent and acceptance of charity from the United States as especially harmful to national prestige. In Afghanistan, on the other hand, I have found considerable anxiety about what was termed the cultural pollution which follows western aid and the development of tourism. One can only sympathize with these qualms.

Conservationists tend in general to be apolitical and international in outlook, viewing the problems with which they wrestle on a world-wide rather than a national basis; but they are not exempt from the doubts or attitudes of the people they are trying to help. Those from the west who work in the Third World learn to be patient with accusations of scientific imperialism, however unjust these may be. Those who succeed learn to teach unobtrusively, to encourage local initiative and to give the credit for their achievements to the people with whom they are working.

My Indian friends are familiar with these problems and have always treated me with kindness. They are working hard to dispel the élitist image of conservation and are wisely concentrating on the creation of hundreds of wildlife youth clubs, as part of the educational programme of the World Wildlife Fund. Young people in every country have more idealism and a quicker grasp of the need to protect the natural environment than their elders. The youth clubs are a great success, as they have been in Africa, and are now beginning to spread into the rural areas, where they are perhaps needed most. Maybe in time they will reach the *maldharis* and even the untouchable *harijans*.

As this book goes to press, the outlook for the Gir lions is encouraging. Their population is again rising and has passed the 200 mark. Not all the *maldharis* have yet been withdrawn, but more than half of them have gone and all cattle have been excluded. Their exodus has already resulted in a remarkable improvement in the vegetation, to which the prey-species of the lions have responded by a veritable population explosion. The latest census shows that the reserve now contains 4500 chital, 1500 nilgai, nearly 1000 four-horned antelope, 706 sambur, 195 chinkara and about 2000 wild boar. Never before have the lions been faced with such bountiful resources and even the leopards have increased to 155. The area of the completely protected inner sanctum has been increased to 100 square miles and in 1975 the Indian Board for Wildlife voted the Gir the best managed reserve in the country. There is every prospect that when the national park is fully functioning it will become one of the most important in India.

My contribution had been a small one. I had had the good fortune to be there at the right time to synthesize the work of my predecessors, both Indian and foreign, and to have written a report at a propitious moment.

IO

A JEWEL IN THE OCEAN

I WAS fortunate to have made my first visit to the Seychelles archipelago just before the completion of the jumbo-jet airport on Mahé, which was to have such a profound effect on its future. They were dredging thousands of tons of dead coral from the sea to make up the runway at the time and giant earth-moving equipment was crawling all over the promontory. I could imagine what was in store for the sleepy, lotus-eating Seychellois watching from under the palm trees.

I made two circuits of the islands, landing by rubber dinghy on eight of the larger ones. At that time the Seychelles were still a very remote British Crown Colony, which few people had ever visited. During the first half of the nineteenth century Mahé, which has a fine natural harbour, had had some importance for coaling the ships on the way to India, but with the opening of the Suez Canal it sank back with a grateful sigh into obscurity again. Its people were happy and though poor, reasonably self-sufficient. What did they want of the modern world?

When the chattering tourists poured out of the belly of the first big jet plane which landed in 1971, everything changed. Almost overnight this exquisitely beautiful group of islands in the middle of the Indian Ocean, halfway between East Africa and Bombay, became the new Mecca for the wealthy tourists of the world. A second airstrip was built on the island of Praslin; later two more were built on

Bird Island and Frégate. There was a frantic rush to build hotels, many of which were occupied even before they were completed. Within five short years the coast of Mahé within reach of Victoria, the picturesque capital of the archipelago, began to conform to the standard pattern of touristic development which is so familiar in the Caribbean, the Mediterranean and many of the Pacific holiday resorts. The speculators waxed rich and the Seychellois natives who had lounged beneath the coconut palms or fished in the sparkling blue lagoons found new employment as smartly uniformed waiters or chambermaids in the glossy new hotels, where they grumbled about the new tempo of life in their once peaceful homeland. The Seychelles are still almost unbelievably beautiful, but, alas, not everywhere. There are now half a dozen new hotels on Mahé. Fortunately they are mostly of modest size and are not unsightly. I learned during a recent visit that at least three more are to be built, one of which will have 700 rooms. It would be idle to pretend that an edifice of this size, with its attendant crowds, will not harm the tranquillity of the island, nor increase the already rising coastal pollution. Thus far, however, the government had succeeded in keeping the tourist expansion under reasonable control.

The ninety-two islands of the archipelago, which include the Amirante and Cosmoledo groups, are scattered like a broken necklace over a great expanse of the Indian Ocean. They are mostly of very ancient granite, some fringed with coral reefs. Mahé is the largest and is mountainous, rising steeply from the sea, with two peaks, the higher of which, Morne Seychellois, is just under 3000 feet. The climate is heavenly and there is no risk from the hurricanes which cause such devastation to the Mascarenes to the south.

The Portuguese were apparently the first discoverers of the Seychelles, which appear on a map drawn by Alberto Cantino in 1501, though no landings were made. The earliest recorded landings were those of the fourth English East Indies Company expedition in 1609, when the crews of HMS *Ascension* and HMS *Good Hope* went ashore on Mahé

E

and North Island. They were unable to identify the islands, however, and it was left to Rear-Admiral Sir William Warton a hundred years later to do so from examination of the detailed report written by John Jordain, who had been a member of the expedition. Jordain's report was admirably detailed. It speaks of 'the plentiful coker nutts and much fish and fowles' and of the numerous 'tortells' (giant tortoises) which the men could 'kill at pleasure with staves'. It also mentions the many enormous 'allagartes' (alligators) with which the islands abounded, but these were, of course, crocodiles. The text-books on the Seychelles say the species was the Nile crocodile, normally a freshwater species, but as they often occurred at sea between the islands, one wonders if perhaps they were more probably the big seafaring estuarine crocodiles.

Jordain's report was enthusiastic about the immense trees in the lowland forest of Mahé, which he described as 'very bigge and straight as an arrow for seventy feet without sprigge except at the top'. These were probably the valuable ironwoods *Vateria seychellarium*, which used to grow to 190 feet until the lowland forests, like the crocodiles, the giant tortoises and the dugongs of the Seychelles, were completely destroyed by the settlers in the nineteenth century.

The French annexed the islands in 1742 and created the first settlements there in 1768, with the object of challenging the Dutch monopoly of the spice trade. A multitude of tropical vegetation was introduced, but the only spices to survive commercially have been cinnamon and vanilla. In 1814 the islands were ceded to Britain, but by then the French influence was so strongly rooted that both the *Code Napoléon* and the créole patois, based on French but with a mixture of Indian, Bantu and English, were maintained. The Seychelles became an independent republic in 1975, with an economy based firmly on tourism.

Inevitably, two centuries of human settlement have damaged the wildlife of the islands, quite apart from the introduction of alien species. Their large animals have disappeared, except for the handsome orange-breasted fox-bat, but there are still some unique smaller creatures such as the tiger chameleon and various caecilians, skinks and lizards. Three of the endemic birds have become extinct and six or seven of the remaining endemic species have become extreme rarities. The three birds now most numerous on Mahé are 'foreigners' – the Indian mynah, the Madagascar fody and the little barred ground dove, which originated in Australia; all of these have become enthusiastic parasites at tourist meal tables. Some 500 plant species have been identified, of which no fewer than eighty are unique. These include one extreme rarity – the curious 'jelly-fish plant', a veritable prehistoric relic, of which only half a dozen examples are known to exist on Mahé. Much of the vegetation is mixed with introductions, though the six unique species of palms have survived and the original cloud-forest is still undisturbed above the 1500-foot level on Mahé. In the lowlands most of the great native trees have gone, to make way for cinnamon or tea plantations, while at sea level dense plantations of coconut encircle the islands. The original extensive mangrove swamps which are typical of most Indian Ocean islands and are important to many forms of marine life, reptiles and birds, have now disappeared from Mahé except for one small tract on the west coast.

The Seychelles were somewhat vaguely known to science for many years as the home of a number of unique birds and plants. In 1964–5 the World Wildlife Fund sponsored an expedition to ascertain the true status of wildlife. I was therefore well briefed before arriving there. I knew, for example, that the bare-legged scops owl on Mahé was regarded as one of the rarest birds in the world; I was fortunate enough to see one, thus becoming only the fourth living person to have done so. I knew also that the black paradise flycatcher on La Digue Island was very near to extinction, as were the handsome magpie robin on Frégate Island, the obscure little brush warbler on Cousin and the Seychelles kestrel and black parrot on Praslin. On Bird Island I knew I should find at least one million pairs of sooty terns breeding and on Desnoeufs, in the Amirante group of islands, about twice that number. I had read all about the giant coco-de-mer, with its irresistibly suggestively shaped forty-pound fruit and twenty-foot fan-shaped leaves, which grows only in the beautiful Vallée de Mai on Praslin. The imaginative General Gordon of Khartoum firmly identified Praslin as the original Garden of Eden and the coco-de-mer as the Tree of Knowledge. In fact, the only thing I was completely unprepared for was the enchanting beauty of the islands. This is something one has to experience, for it cannot be adequately described. Guy Lionnet, who used to be Director of Agriculture, and has lived in the Seychelles for more than thirty years, is the only writer I know who has succeeded in giving a rounded impression of the variety of geology, vegetation and wildlife represented in the archipelago.*

As a result of the studies made in 1964–5, some measures of conservation had already been taken before the tourist boom began and before I reached the islands. The British Nature Conservancy had made proposals for the establishment of a number of reserves and parks, the first of which secured the preservation of the Vallée de Mai on Praslin. This is now well managed as a botanical garden and a tourist attraction. La Digue, on which all the speculators had their eyes because of its unique old-world rural charm, was also given protection. Some of the smaller islands of importance to wildlife, however, were privately owned. Because of the peculiar provisions of the French *code civil*, it was extremely difficult either to purchase them or to enforce conservation measures on the owners. One of these was Cousin Island, which was particularly important as the home of a number of very rare endemic birds and other forms of wildlife. I had been involved in the negotiations which later enabled it to be secured as a fully protected reserve and was eager to examine it.

Cousin (it is of course pronounced in the French way) looks from above like a brilliantly green emerald floating on

*Lionnet, Guy, *The Seychelles*, David & Charles, Newton Abbott, 1972.

the surface of the blue ocean. It is roughly circular in shape and one can walk right around it in little more than an hour. There is a hill towards the south-west side, where tumbled rocks emerge from the vegetation, most of which consists of coconut palms or feathery casuarinas, though there are other much more interesting trees and shrubs among them. At low tide, wonderful white sand beaches are exposed. Opposite Cousin is the island of Cousine, also heavily clad with palms, while to the east lies the big island of Praslin.

When my wife and I landed through the surf on to the white beach, we were greeted by Malcolm and Mary Penny, the two young scientists appointed to do research on Cousin's wild inhabitants. With them were their two small boys, as brown as berries and thoroughly enjoying living like Robinson Crusoe on the tiny tropical island. We walked through the graceful casuarina trees, where intensely white fairy terns were sitting in hundreds, precariously balanced on their single eggs or chicks. The eggs were laid without a trace of nesting material on bare branches, on stumps, on fallen palm fronds and even on the narrow edge of the reserve notice-board which proclaimed Cousin as belonging strictly to its birds. Fairy terns are exquisite little seabirds, with large, inquiring black eyes and the daintiest of little black feet, which are un-webbed as an adaptation to their arboreal nesting habit. Some of the tall coconut palms had toe-holes cut at three-foot intervals to enable the Seychellois to climb them and cut down the nuts for making copra. On several such trees the fairy terns sat one above the other in the slots, like tenants in a high-rise apartment house. Mary, who was studying their breeding success, said that many eggs fell from their ridiculously insecure lodgings, or were taken by the large skinks (smooth-skinned lizards) which were scuttling among the vegetation. In consequence, fewer than 25 per cent of the eggs laid produced flying young.

In the centre of the island is an old well, providing a source of fresh water. Beside it we found a huge and obviously very ancient Indian Ocean giant tortoise, one of the fortunate survivors of a once numerous species. Purplish-red turtle doves and intricately barred little ground doves were feeding by the well. Above us a minute sunbird, looking more like a big bee than a bird, darted and chattered in the sunlight. On the sandy track were groups of busy little Madagascan fodys, the males bright scarlet and the females streaky brown. I was anxious to see the unique Seychelles fody, known locally as the 'toq-toq', which is found only on Cousin, Cousine and Frégate; Malcolm soon heard its quiet '*tsk-tsk*' call-note and led me to it. By comparison with the flamboyant Madagascan species, which was introduced into the Seychelles, the endemic bird is a rather drab little grey-brown creature with a touch of gold on the crown and throat. But to any ornithologist, the first sight of an extreme rarity is always exciting. The even more rare Cousin brush-warbler was also soon located and I was impressed by its rich, melodious song, which it repeated as it dodged among the low vegetation. The entire world population of this species is restricted to Cousin Island. In 1968 there were only eighteen pairs; now there are at least 120 pairs.

We walked back to the Pennys' small, palm-thatched house by the shore for a cool drink. Near the door was an old gnarled tree with a hollow base, from which protruded the long white tail-streamer of a tropicbird. Peering in, I could see the single chick, a fat ball of grey down. Its mother, beautifully barred with black and white, threatened me with her huge scarlet bill, but refused to leave the nest.

We then walked around the island shore, where thousands of terns – noddy, lesser noddy, bridled, crested and sooty – were wheeling above the surf. A dozen or more species of small waders were feeding at the water's edge, among them several big, heavy-billed crab plovers and green-backed herons. All along the shore lesser noddies were nesting in the palms and casuarinas. They are sleek, sooty-brown, with pale crowns, whereas the noddies have elegant white caps like the wigs worn by barristers. By comparison with the fairy terns, both noddies are much more like the European species in their noisy and aggressive behaviour, though they allowed us to approach their nests closely. Three species of ghost crabs occupy the beaches and find plentiful food by preying on fallen nestlings and the newly emerged young of the hawksbill turtles which lay their eggs here.

On our second visit to Cousin, Malcolm and Mary invited us to supper. When Mary and my wife had put the children to bed, Malcolm took us up the hill to watch the shearwaters returning to their nests, which they do only in darkness. It was already dark when we set out and we carried torches. Cousin at night is almost as fascinating as it is by day. Strange and beautiful moths flitted through the beams of our torches and every now and then we picked out fairy terns on their eggs or young, sitting like little gleaming white porcelain statuettes. Dozens of five-inch millipedes marched across the sandy track, their tiny legs moving in rhythmic waves beneath their fat, shiny bodies. In the trees, the roosting noddies kept up an almost continuous subdued conversation among themselves, like old women gossiping after an evening church service.

When we finally scrambled to the rocky summit, we could hear the strange groaning and gibbering of the hidden shearwaters deep in their holes. We sat on the warm, eroded granite rocks listening to them and to the soothing obbligato of the surf on the shore below. Above us the sky was blazing with stars, the constellations all looking bigger and brighter than they ever do in Europe. There was a splendour about the night which was almost preposterous. An American or perhaps Russian satellite winged its lonely way below the stars, signalling back to earth the latest information about the weather, or maybe transmitting pictures of military importance.

Presently Malcolm said: 'Here they come', and something glided past us silently and dived into the rocks. In the beams of our torches we could soon pick out dozens of narrow-winged shearwaters flying in from the ocean to relieve their mates. Some landed almost at our feet and scuttled quickly into their hidden nest-holes by tobogganing on their breasts, their thin legs being too weak to enable them to walk upright.

Two species nest on Cousin, the wedge-tailed, of which there are about 30000 pairs and the Audubon's, only a few hundreds of which are known to breed here.

The sheer mass of birds on this tiny island is really extraordinary. There are 100000 pairs of lesser noddy terns, 10000 pairs of fairy terns and 3000 common noddy, all breeding in dense proximity to each other. During the height of the nesting period, the total number of birds of all kinds which are crammed into Cousin's one-tenth of a square mile, from the tree-tops to ground level, reaches a staggering total of 250000. Every part of the island is then vibrant with life.

We returned to find that Mary had somehow contrived to produce an excellent dinner for us, even though her little paraffin refrigerator had broken down. Her shopping, she told us cheerfully, was restricted to visits by out-board *pirogue* to far-away Praslin. Most housewives would have been shocked by the conditions under which the meal had been prepared. The minute kitchen was illuminated by a single hurricane lamp, which Mary carried from room to room. The dining table, however, was lit by candles, around which a cloud of moths and beetles circled. Gecko lizards scuttled continuously over the walls and ceiling, snapping up flies. Millipedes and large beetles trundled across the floor and around our feet. The dinner was nevertheless a huge success and we were delighted to talk to these two young people who knew so much about every aspect of the island's natural history. We were sad to leave them when our dinghy came bobbing through the surf to take us back to the ship, whose bright lights shone across the dark sea where it lay at anchor. It had been a very romantic evening.

I returned to England determined to do all I could to help the International Council for Bird Preservation, in whose hands lay various plans for protecting the rare birds of the Seychelles. The Chairman of the British Section was my old friend and colleague, Professor W. H. Thorpe, F.R.S. Its Secretary, who for many years had been the prime mover in the affairs of the ICPB, was Miss Phyllis Barclay-Smith,

C.B.E. Her many achievements, particularly in promoting international legislation, have earned her a reputation second to none among conservationists.

In the spring of 1967 a meeting was arranged between Professor Thorpe and Phyllis Barclay-Smith, representing the ICPB, and Peter Scott and myself representing the World Wildlife Fund, to discuss the possibility of purchasing Cousin from its owner, Madame Jumeau, who was represented by her legal adviser, Sir Peter Agnew. The owner was willing to sell, though the price asked was a high one – some £16500 including the legal fees involved. Nevertheless, although such a sum was not available, we felt that the importance of the island merited the risk of accepting the offer. Having myself been signatory on behalf of the WWF to the purchase of the Coto Doñana reserve in Spain for £300000 with the hope that we could raise the money in time (which we did) I felt sure we could take a similar risk to save Cousin. I was right. Thanks to a vigorous joint fund-raising campaign by the ICPB and the WWF, the sum was raised by the required date. It was a great international effort, with generous donations coming from the United States and the Netherlands and from countries as far apart as Tasmania, South Africa and France. The bulk of the money, however, was raised in Great Britain, where two of the WWF branches, in Eastbourne and Birmingham, played the leading part. Lectures, garden parties, raffles and school competitions were organized by many private individuals. The campaign would not have been such a success had it not been for Tony Beamish, who had made two superb colour films, *The Isles of Eden* and *Follow the Wind to Cousin*, which enabled people to appreciate the real beauty and interest of the islands. The close-ups of the fairy terns on Cousin were certain winners and the audiences responded enthusiastically to the suggestion that they should buy a small plot on the island at a proposed price and donate the land to the organizers.

The moment the purchase of Cousin was completed and control of the island placed in the hands of the ICBP, a

strong local committee was formed in the Seychelles, under
the chairmanship of M. Philippe Loustau-Lalanne of the
Department of Agriculture, who became the Honorary
Representative of the ICBP. Arrangements were made to
have the island guarded. The few domestic pigs were
removed and the cropping of the hawksbill turtles and fat
nestling shearwaters made illegal. The monthly cropping of
coconuts for copra was permitted to continue as it in no way
interfered with the wildlife and provided a modest income
for labour. Tourist visits were restricted to three days a week
in order to minimize disturbance. Within a year there were
nevertheless 1370 visitors from thirty-eight different countries. Since then the accommodation for the scientists working on the island has been greatly improved and in 1974 a
small, but well-equipped, laboratory was donated by Professor Rudolph Geigy, one of the Trustees of the WWF.

I had discussed with Malcolm Penny the obvious advantage of securing Cousine Island as well as Cousin. Its close
proximity would provide an admirable basis for comparative
studies. Moreover, the risk of it falling into the hands of
speculators posed a serious problem and could have disastrous consequences to the tranquillity of the reserve. Soon
after my visit, Tony Beamish and Roger Tory Peterson
arrived at Cousin on the *Lindblad Explorer*, accompanying a
group of tourists. They, too, were impressed by the potential
importance of Cousine and started a fund for its acquisition.
The ICBP quickly opened negotiations with the owner of the
island, but the price asked, inflated by the growing touristic
development of the Seychelles, was far beyond the possibi-
lities of fund-raising. Cousine was bought at an even higher
price by a German. Professor Thorpe at once wrote to him,
offering the services of the ICPB in preserving the wildlife
of the island. By good fortune the new owner proved to be
interested in birds and made an amicable arrangement to
maintain the island as a virtually undisturbed complement
to Cousin.

The progress of conservation in the Seychelles in the last
few years has been a remarkable story of wisdom and success.

This has been brought about by close co-operation between the government (both old and new), the ICBP and the WWF. A marine national park now protects the vulnerable coral reefs, tropical fish and crustaceans around St Anne's Island. Some at least of the original cloud-forest in the highlands seems likely to survive now that Morne Seychellois has become a reserve. The endemic wildlife of the Vallée de Mai on Praslin is well protected. Christopher Cadbury, who played an important part in the acquisition of Cousin, generously purchased Aride Island in 1973 in order to protect its wildlife. La Digue with its precious paradise fly-catchers is now wardened by the ICBP, and Bird Island and Frégate have also been given a satisfactory degree of safety, in spite of the airstrips which have been built on them. Cousine remains reasonably undisturbed and Cousin has become a world famous island for science.

Sooner or later it was inevitable that the Seychelles, whose islands have such outstanding beauty and such obvious potentiality for tourism, would be developed for this purpose. In economic terms, the benefits to the Seychellois are enormous. Fortunately in this instance it was possible for conservationists to act quickly enough to work in co-operation with the local authorities to anticipate and control the more obvious excesses which normally accompany a sudden tourist boom. The Seychelles government White Paper entitled *Conservation Policy in the Seychelles* defined an admirable programme, which included the creation of national parks and a National Parks and Nature Conservancy Commission. Not all its provisions have yet been implemented, however, and some may be too late. Nevertheless, the future for the conservation of wildlife in the new republic is one of the interests of the President, Mr Albert René, who fully recognizes its importance to the world of science and to the Seychellois. He and his ministers are aware of the risks which their dependence on tourism involves. They will not allow the natural treasures of the islands to be lost by the indifference or negligence which have occurred in so many other archipelagos.

How good it is to remember that thousands of people in many countries, who will probably never set eyes on the Seychelles, were willing to give money so that Cousin, the crown jewel of the archipelago, could avoid such risks! Had Cousin not attracted wide international interest it is doubtful that the Seychelles government would have embarked with such readiness on its now very extensive conservation programme.

11

THE PREHISTORIC RELIC

ONE day when I was sitting in a Land-Rover on the Buligi track, which follows the Albert Nile to its confluence with the Victoria Nile in the beautiful Murchison Falls National Park, a rhinoceros and her recently born calf emerged from the scrub. Being up-wind from me and having no red-billed oxpeckers riding on her back to give the alarm, she paid no attention to my stationary vehicle and began cropping the grass. The calf, an engaging little creature, kept close to its mother's enormous head, looking about with evident interest at the long-faced Jackson's hartebeestes grazing near by.

A baby rhino weighs no less than seventy-five pounds at birth, but by comparison with its mother, twelve feet long and weighing three and a half tons, the one I was watching looked minute. They were white rhinos. The Murchison Falls is one of the few places where both the white and the black species can be seen together. The black rhino is a much more restless and irascible beast, which does not hesitate to charge intruding vehicles like a run-away tank. The white is more placid, but one has to be careful nevertheless if it has a small calf with it. It is no more white than the black is black: both are dark grey, though the white has a paler skin. Both have two horns. The name 'white' is derived from the Afrikaans *weit*, meaning wide and referring to the square lip which makes it an efficient grazer. The black, of which there are perhaps 10000 to 12000, chiefly in Uganda and Kenya, have a pointed muzzle and a long, prehensile lip suited to its habit of browsing on shrubs and twigs.

I could not help feeling, as I watched the rhino, that all five species, two in Africa and three in Asia, must be nearing the end of their evolutionary line. There had been rhinoceros-like creatures on Earth more than fifty million years before man became a bipedal animal. They are related to the tapirs; their common original ancestor was probably the gigantic, tapir-like Baluchiterum, which stood eighteen feet at the shoulder. A full-grown rhino can tip the scales at nearly four tons and, next to the elephant, is the second largest surviving land mammal. This tremendous weight, combined with short legs and very poor eyesight, would make it extremely vulnerable to predators but for the protection of its massive hide. However, sheer size and weight did not save the dinosaurs, which once dominated the animal kingdom, but were their undoing. Nevertheless, until the belief emerged in China and neighbouring countries that the ground-up horn of a rhinoceros was a powerful aphrodisiac, all five of today's species, though obviously such prehistoric creatures, had been thriving. It was this quite erroneous belief and the very high prices paid for the horns which were now driving them towards extinction.

All three Asiatic species are listed as gravely endangered. Unlike their African relatives, they have distinctively 'armour-plated' hides hanging in heavy folds around the neck, shoulders and hindquarters, dotted with numerous prominent tubercles resembling rivet-heads. The Indian and Javan species are single-horned, while the smaller Sumatran rhino has two stumpy horns and a smoother, less folded hide; when immature, its hide is hairy. The total number of the Indian species surviving is about 1100, of which 660 are in the Kaziranga National Park in Assam, 300 in the Chitawan National Park in Nepal, and small numbers in the Manas reserve in Assam and the Jaldapara in northern West Bengal.

The desperate efforts which have been made to save the last of the Javan rhinos in the Udjung Kulon Reserve in western Java provide a remarkable story of perseverance in the face of innumerable difficulties. The terrain favoured by these elusive animals is extremely dense and swampy rain-forest. Visibility is restricted to a very few yards and the physical effort required in searching for evidence of their presence, such as browsed saplings, tracks, droppings or mud wallows, is daunting in the prevailing heat and humidity. The local native poachers are of course much better able to overcome these difficulties than either the Indonesian or western scientists who for many years have striven to protect the few surviving animals. Between 1963 and 1966 the population of rhinos suffered particularly heavy losses to the poachers. In 1967 Professor Dr Rudolf Schenkel and his wife, Dr Lotte Schenkel-Hulliger of the Zoological Institute of Basle, carried out a detailed study for the World Wildlife Fund and made a number of practical recommendations. The system of guarding the reserve was plainly ineffective and the poorly-paid guards were terrified of the well-armed poachers. Nothing short of a fully trained and disciplined guard force armed with modern weapons could hope to get the upper hand.

From that time onward the WWF has given high priority to making the reserve and its guard force fully effective. The Indonesian authorities have co-operated enthusiastically. The Ministry of Agriculture at Djakarta, who are responsible for Indonesia's rapidly expanding conservation programme throughout the enormous archipelago, were, however, very short of funds. A series of projects connected with the Udjung Kulon Reserve has therefore been funded by the WWF. These included the provision of housing and guard-huts, uniforms, weapons, medical supplies and other equipment for the guards. In order that they should work full-time under the prevailing arduous conditions, their wages were supplemented and they were given special training in shooting and tracking. Vehicles and boats were provided to enable them to concentrate quickly when a raid was in progress. Finally a field research station was erected for the use of visiting scientists. One of the latest projects has been to increase the food sources for the rhinos, by extensive planting of saplings of preferred species. All these activities have been carefully supervised by the Schenkels, who are now recognized as the world's leading authorities on the Javan rhino. Their efforts have been well rewarded. In spite of the continuing activities of the highly organized poachers, the rhino population has recovered, from about twenty-five in 1967 to forty-eight or fifty by 1977. They are the only ones left in the world. The reserve itself has recently been enlarged by another 10000 hectares.

The Sumatran, the smallest of the rhinos, is also under great pressure. The species is thought to have about twenty left in Burma, fifteen in Thailand, twenty-five in Malaysia and forty in the Gunung Leuser Reserve in Sumatra. All three Asian species, though now strictly protected, are constantly harassed by poachers, the current value of a rhino carcass on the black market being about £1000 or more. Every part of the animal has a commercial value – the hide, the hair, the blood, the nails, the internal organs, the urine and, of course, the horn. One can buy rhino urine from many Indian zoos as a 'cure' for asthma. Cups carved from the horn are supposed to disintegrate if a jealous spouse is trying to administer poison in the drink. These curious beliefs in the magical properties of the rhinoceros are still firmly entrenched.

The killing of a rhinoceros in order to hack off a few pounds of compacted hair (for this is all the 'horn' really is) is like knocking down a great cathedral merely in order to steal the cross on its spire. The custom is not only barbarous, but a lasting shame on the countries of the Far East which perpetuate it. As HRH Prince Philip once said at a dinner in New York: 'For all the good it does them, they might just as well grind up the leg of a kitchen chair', a remark which incidentally resulted in a diplomatic protest, incredible though this may seem.

Rhinos are, of course, also protected in all African reserves and national parks where they occur. The number of licences issued for shooting them elsewhere is now very small and they are expensive. A certain number of rhinos are

The rarest of the five rhinoceros species is the forest-dwelling Javan. In the Udjung Kulon Reserve numbers have increased from only twenty-eight in 1967 to about fifty.

A tiger takes a siesta. Saving the tiger from the threat of extinction was one of the World Wildlife Fund's most successful international efforts.

Opposite above: Poachers using foot-snares kill thousands of rhinoceroses in Africa to satisfy the Asian demand for the ground-up horn as a supposed aphrodisiac.

Opposite below: As the price of ivory increases, so does the volume of commercially sponsored poaching of elephants, which in Africa is now on an immense scale.

The magnificent California condor has a wing-span of nearly ten feet. Though one of the most carefully protected birds in America, only forty survive.

The noisy scrub-bird of Australia was believed to be extinct. When a small colony was re-discovered near Perth, Prince Philip asked for its protection.

killed by the more courageous tribes such as the Masai and Acholi, who are brave enough to spear them as proof of manhood. A cloud of vultures had led me to the carcass of a black rhino speared by the Masai in the carefully guarded Ngoro-Ngoro reserve just before I reached the Murchison Falls. But the real slaughter in Africa is by wire foot-snares, which are laid in thousands wherever rhinos are present. Wire is cheap and readily available, even if it has to be cut from telephone poles, or extracted from old lorry tyres. The nooses are quickly laid and easily concealed. Usually they are tethered to a heavy log, which the rhino drags through the bush until exhausted, its foot almost severed by the wire. Elephants are trapped in the same manner, but are often caught by their questing trunks, which are not infrequently thus amputated by the weight of the log.

The cruelty involved in trapping is appalling and the losses prodigious. In 1976, when by a sudden political decision the Kenyan government allowed its fine national parks service virtually to collapse, the immediate result was that large numbers of elephants and rhinos in the immense Tsavo National Park were slaughtered for their ivory or horn by poachers. Mombasa is the main port of exit for this contraband, which then goes by boat to traders in the Far East, chiefly through Singapore, Hong Kong and Japan. Well-armed Somalis, equipped with lorries and automatic weapons, added to the slaughter in northern Kenya. The most recent reports put the losses of elephants alone by poaching or drought at between 12000 and 18000 *in one year*.* When one recalls the highly efficient state of the national parks service in Kenya in the days of Archie Ritchie and Mervyn Cowie and the annual income of millions of pounds from tourists which the parks used to earn, one can only describe the situation as a tragedy for Kenya.

The Murchison Falls National Park in Uganda, however, continued to thrive. Its history is one of which conserva-

---

*The number of elephants killed world-wide was of course far greater: in 1975 Hong Kong alone imported a tonnage of tusks representing the loss of 30000 Indian and African elephants. By weight, the price of ivory is now four times that of gold

tionists can be proud. It began its existence as the much
smaller Bunyoro-Gulu Game Reserve in the days when the
late Captain Charles Pitman was Chief Game Warden of
Uganda. The area was then chiefly known for its elephants,
which were some of the mightiest tuskers in Africa, though
poachers have since then greatly reduced their numbers.
Chief credit for its later enlargement and classification as a
national park belongs to Major Bruce Kinloch, who succeeded Pitman as Chief Game Warden. The area it now
embraces, which of course includes the spectacular falls,
where the Victoria Nile is squeezed by the rocks into a
twenty-foot-wide stupendous waterfall, is now 1557 square
miles – a little larger than the whole of Hampshire. The park
contains some sixty-five species of mammals and more than
400 species of birds. It also has the largest surviving population of crocodiles to be found anywhere in Africa. In its
Rabongo Forest region there are even some chimpanzees,
though they are not easily found. The boat trip from the
Paraa Lodge to the foot of the falls provides an extraordinary panorama of wildlife on the banks of the river. In
the deep pools below the falls there is spectacular sport-
fishing, with Nile perch of up to 200 pounds. Although perhaps lacking the extravaganza of the spectacle provided
when tens of thousands of wildebeestes and zebras are
migrating across the plains of the Serengeti National Park,
the Murchison is very hard to beat when it comes to variety
of scenery and wildlife.

By the end of 1969 the Murchison had become one of the
biggest money-spinners in Africa and indeed was often overcrowded in the tourist areas. In Africa, however, one can
never be sure that a good thing will last. In 1970 the astonished world learned that the Ugandan government had
decided to build a colossal dam and hydro-electric installation which would cover the falls and their surroundings with
concrete. It would, of course, take several years to build,
but hundreds of giant earth-moving juggernauts would
speedily destroy the national park. Dr Milton Obote's
government proudly announced that as the power produced

by this glorious scheme would be far beyond Uganda's needs, the surplus energy would be sold to neighbouring countries.

There was, of course, immediate uproar in the conservation world, led by Bruce Kinloch and Francis Katete, the Ugandan Director of National Parks, a man very highly regarded by all conservationists. Sadly, Francis Katete was killed in a car crash very soon afterwards, but by then the World Wildlife Fund and the IUCN were in full cry to prevent the scheme from being implemented. Expert civil engineers were engaged, who quickly showed that several satisfactory alternative sites existed for the dam and that the expected revenue from the sale of surplus energy would, in any event, be less than that obtainable from the park as a tourist attraction. Efforts were made to convince the World Bank that finance should be withheld unless an alternative site was selected. Leading newspapers and broadcasters strongly supported the conservationist view.

To no avail – the Ugandan government, like many others before it, saw the plan in a rosy haze of *folie de grandeur*, as something to bring it fame and international respect. To some politicians, the bigger the project the more irresistible it becomes. Then, as sometimes happens when all seems lost, salvation came from a totally unexpected quarter. The burly figure of General Idi Amin sprang into the limelight. He staged a military *coup d'état*, overthrew the government and became the new President of Uganda. One of his first decisions was to cancel the Murchison Falls project, partly for sound economic reasons, but doubtless also because of the opprobrium being heaped on Uganda by the international press concerning the impending destruction of the world-famous falls.

The white rhinoceroses in the park (now in deference to nationalism re-named the Kabalega Falls National Park) are part of a remarkable conservation story. The species had not been identified as distinct from the black rhinoceros until 1817, when a specimen shot by William Burchell in the Karroo in South Africa was scientifically examined and named. For nearly a hundred years the white rhino was thought to exist only in southern Africa. Around the turn of the century, however, an English hunter named Cotton identified what appeared to be the same species in central Africa, nearly 2000 miles north of the Karroo. He was allowed to claim it as a new species, on the grounds of its wide geographical separation from the South African population and some minor differences in the skull and teeth. It was named Cotton's rhinoceros, though in fact only a race of the southern species. By 1906 the northern race had been identified in the Central African Republic, southern Sudan, Uganda, Zaire and Rwanda, but its numbers were declining fast. In 1961 a dozen of the survivors were captured and, with financial assistance from the World Wildlife Fund and Anglia Television, were transferred as a precaution to the protection of the Murchison Falls National Park. Tribal wars and revolutions accelerated the destruction of the remainder of the northern race, nearly 1000 of them being killed by rebels in the Garamba National Park alone during the Congo revolution. By 1970 only about 300 remained, scattered between southern Sudan and Lake Tchad. It is feared that most of these have since been killed or have died from natural causes. Apart from the original number moved to the Murchison Park, 'Cotton's rhinoceros' may now be extinct.

Meanwhile, in the southern part of Africa, where during the last century the white rhino had once been common throughout a huge area, the homesteaders and hunters had also been busy exterminating it. By 1906 it was thought to be extinct everywhere except for a group of between thirty and fifty in the Umfolozi Game Reserve in Zululand, under the protection of the Natal Parks Board. That the white rhinoceros still exists at all in Africa is entirely due to the great care and skill with which the Natal Parks Board then began looking after its precious survivors. They were guarded more carefully than any South African gold mine. Nobody was allowed anywhere near them and the staff were forbidden to tell anyone how many were in the reserve. It was, in fact, not until 1959 that the outside world was permitted to know that the tiny original population had been increased to about 600 healthy white rhinos. It was an almost unbelievable achievement, which conservationists in other parts of the world greeted with admiration and astonishment.

Thanks to the ideal conditions and highly skilled management at Umfolozi, the white rhinos repaid their saviours during the following five years by indulging in a positive population explosion, their numbers rising to 1600. By then, of course, the reserve was too small to hold such a number and the decision was taken to begin re-stocking the areas where the species formerly used to exist in southern and central Africa. But only where properly protected reserves or national parks existed.

Today the white rhinoceros is a familiar sight in many African countries. All of them originated from the Umfolozi herd. Small numbers were carefully transported and released in reserves in Kenya, the Sudan, Uganda, Angola, Rhodesia, Mozambique, Botswana, South-West Africa and various parts of southern Africa.

To capture and transport a rhinoceros weighing three or four tons is no simple matter. In 1960, however, Dr A. M. Harthoorn developed the now widely used dart-gun, using the tranquillizing drug M.99, followed by its antidote, Lethidrone, which was injected into the rhino's ear to arouse it just sufficiently to enable it to be walked into a travelling cage. This is an operation requiring great skill and very exact control. Some of the rhinos were lifted by helicopter, the remainder by truck and plane.

The total number of re-introductions of the southern white rhino into other countries, plus their subsequent offspring, is now in the region of 700 animals. At Umfolozi itself and in the adjacent Hluhluwe Reserve, the breeding stock is being maintained at around 1300. There are, in addition, about 500 in private game reserves or running wild on local farms. Many more have been sent to zoos and safari parks in various parts of the world, including the fine herd which visitors now enjoy seeing while riding the aptly named

Umfolozi Miniature Railway at the Whipsnade branch of the London Zoo.

One of the heart-warming aspects of the achievement at Umfolozi was the decision of the Natal Parks Board to take no profit from the return of their surplus rhinos to their original habitat in other countries. The importing countries have to pay only for the transportation costs. Saving the white rhinoceros from the brink of extinction and seeing its name removed from the IUCN *Red Data Book* of endangered mammals has been considered a sufficient reward.

12

TIGER, TIGER, BURNING BRIGHT

MY obsession about the survival of tigers began in Nepal. That it became an obsession I freely admit and my friends in the conservation movement had to put up with my constant nagging until something was done about it. I did not enjoy the role of gadfly to my colleagues. Even so, had I not pursued the matter relentlessly we should almost certainly have been too late.

In the 1920s there were still at least 100000 tigers in Asia. By 1969 barely 5000 survived, in small groups scattered over the huge continent. It was quite obvious that at such a rate of loss the only tigers left in another twenty years would be those in zoos.

The reasons for this catastrophe were not difficult to identify. The tiger is a forest animal and the forests of Asia were being destroyed at ever-accelerating speed. Secondly, the tiger was the prime target for every sportsman throughout the world. Thirdly, tiger-skin coats and rugs were selling for as much as £3000 and the fur-traders were actively stimulating the shooting, trapping and poisoning of tigers wherever they still existed. This fatal combination, unless checked, would inevitably lead to the final extinction of the species.

Some people argued that tigers were dangerous carnivores which destroyed village cattle and, worse still, sometimes killed villagers. There were plenty of tigers in zoos and wasn't this the best place for them? This argument ignored two important facts. First that the tiger, at the apex of the wild-life pyramid, plays a vital role as the primary predator on deer and wild pigs in Asia, killing the old and sickly and thus maintaining the virility of their wild populations. Where tigers have already been exterminated, farmers are now suffering severe losses from the consequential population explosion of deer and pigs which destroy their crops. Second, that tigers usually take to killing cattle only when their natural prey is scarce, for example when hunters have shot all the deer and pigs near villages. As for man-eaters, obviously when this situation arises the only solution is to shoot the culprit; but almost invariably such animals are found on examination to have been prevented from hunting their natural prey by injury or old age. To put this problem in perspective, the number of deaths caused by man-eating tigers, regrettable though they are, is a tiny fraction of those arising from snake-bites and is infinitesimal compared with fatal traffic accidents or natural calamities in Asia.

As for the argument that the best place for tigers is in zoos, this is clearly specious. Following the growth of public awareness of the threats to wildlife, it has become fashionable for zoos and 'safari parks' to claim that by keeping animals in captivity they are 'saving endangered species from extinction'. With some notable exceptions, this is untrue. Really valuable work of this kind has certainly been done by the zoos in London, Basle, Frankfurt, Phoenix and San Diego, some of which I have mentioned in this book. Such zoos have high scientific standards and not only exchange breeding stocks in order to minimize in-breeding, but keep sperm-banks of endangered animals. Moreover, they no longer collect rare species. A few private collections have also made important contributions to conservation, such as the Duke of Bedford's unique herd of Père David's deer, a species which no longer survives in the wild. However, a great many zoos, 'safari parks' and private collectors, far from saving endangered species, simply make money by exhibiting animals as public entertainment, though they also have an admitted educational value. The great expansion in the number of such establishments represents a continuing drain on vulnerable wild populations and encourages commercial collecting.

The tiger in the wild is active at night, covering many miles while hunting. During the heat of day it lies in the shade near its kill and almost invariably has a swim in the river, where it likes to lie half-submerged for long periods. In most zoos its exercise is limited to six paces either way in an iron and concrete cage and it is deprived entirely of its pastime of swimming. It is also deprived of its main occupation of hunting. Lacking everything it enjoys in life except food, a tiger in captivity becomes lethargic and develops progressive cerebral degeneration, which is increasingly made evident by in-breeding. Its normally acute senses of smell and sight also degenerate. Tigers breed readily in zoos, though the tigress often neglects or eats her new-born cubs; many, therefore, have to be bottle-fed. In the wild a tigress teaches her young to hunt, a process which takes two years before they acquire the skill to pull down and kill a large animal such as the gaur jungle bison, only after which are they able to live independently. Obviously in captivity these skills can never be taught. One often hears that zoos intend to return surplus captive-bred tigers to the wild, but this has never been done. Such animals would be incapable of hunting wild prey and would either starve, be killed by other tigers, or be obliged to take easy prey such as domestic cattle or villagers. No, zoos are emphatically not the answer to the survival of the tiger. If all the wild population were exterminated, what remained in zoos would at best be mere caricatures of the original species, as indeed many zoo tigers are already.

I did not see a wild tiger until the early 1960s. I was riding an elephant at the time, in the Kanha reserve in Madhya Pradesh. The tiger rose from its kill by a stream and circled majestically past my stationary animal, to settle for a siesta in a patch of sunlit grass barely sixty feet from me. Its grace of movement and the shining, silken quality of its coat impressed me instantly as differing entirely from the sluggish, dull-coated tigers I had seen in zoos. The tiger watched me speculatively for a moment and then lowered its massive head and calmly dozed. Even the click of my camera was ignored; but when my elephant, which was rumbling its displeasure at the proximity of the great cat, moved forwards, it slipped sinuously away. From that time onward I was enamoured of tigers.

In 1968 I went camping in Nepal with Peter Byrne, a big-game hunter turned conservationist. We had driven from India across the unmarked frontier into the far western terai, the lowland forest which stretches the length of Nepal below the Himalayas. It was dark when we drove through the trees to the Bamhani river, where Peter's Sherpa servant soon had a fire going and a stew of goat's meat bubbling in the pot. The district was called Sukla Phanta and we were a great distance from civilization.

After supper we sat cross-legged by the fire with a bottle of Scotch, talking about the local wildlife, which Peter knew intimately. It was good tiger-country, but Indian poachers were taking a heavy toll and Peter was pessimistic about the future. All of Nepal's wildlife was declining. There were almost no blackbuck left and only about forty wild buffaloes. Tigers, leopards, snow leopards, red pandas and musk deer would disappear soon. Even the one-horned rhinoceroses in the Chitawan reserve were being heavily poached for the supposed aphrodisiac value of their horns. Sukla Phanta had at that time one of the largest concentrations of the big barasingha swamp deer left in the subcontinent – about 800 of them; but, when the new east–west highway was completed, the region would be open to exploitation and the deer would be lost. Peter felt strongly that it should be turned into a protected reserve.

We slept that night under a canvas top-and-back shelter to keep off the heavy dew and were lulled to sleep by the comfortable, deep honking of frogs down by the river. In the small hours I heard a tiger roar – a wonderful sound which made my spine tingle. Later I was awakened by the loud throaty calling of a hidden forest eagle owl, but otherwise slept soundly. At dawn the jungle was ringing with the cries of hornbills, parakeets and various monkeys. We walked down to the river while breakfast was being prepared and watched a host of egrets, cranes and kingfishers feeding. From time to time peafowl passed overhead on whirring wings, the males trailing their long trains behind them. On the way back I noticed fresh tiger pug-marks on the sand.

'A tigress,' Peter corrected me, indicating the distance between the impress of the toes and the palm, by which the sexes differ. We followed the track, which circled the camp, passing within eight yards of my camp-cot.

'Just curious,' said Peter. 'Probably attracted by the smell of the goat meat.'

After breakfast we waded the Bamhani and explored the luxuriant forest on the far bank, hacking our way through occasional thickets of twenty-foot bamboo and elephant grass. We had fine views of the barasingha, some of the stags carrying fourteen-point antlers. It was exhausting work, however, in the humid heat. After wading a number of muddy, leech-infested streams, I called a halt, to remove my trousers and get rid of the gorged leeches which hung like ripe plums around my waist and legs. While I was lighting my pipe afterwards, we heard something large moving cautiously towards us in the dense vegetation.

'Tiger,' whispered Peter and we froze, listening intently. We were unarmed except for the Gurkha *kukhri* knife hanging from Peter's belt. Silence – then a puffing sigh and the sound of a heavy body crushing down on the dry teak leaves with which the forest was carpeted.

After waiting for a while, Peter whispered, 'Come on, it's probably lying-up after a good meal.' Although my confidence in his knowledge of tigers was great, I could not resist a backward glance as we tiptoed away. Only later, when I had gained experience of tiger-watching in other countries, did I learn how much tigers prefer to avoid contact with man unless openly provoked. I never carried a gun except when studying known man-eaters in the Sunderbans mangrove swamps in Bangladesh.

I returned to England much preoccupied by what Peter had said about the threats to the survival of tigers. The Indian race, whose range included Nepal, was not listed in the IUCN *Red Data Book* of endangered mammals, though several other races were. I decided to make inquiries about the status of all eight races. These were, in descending order of size, the big, long-coated Siberian, which was the progenitor of the species, the Chinese, the Indo-Chinese, the Indian, the Caspian, the Sumatran, the Javan and the Balinese, a tiger smaller by three feet than the Siberian and much more narrowly striped. I wrote to all the experts I could locate in each of these areas. All replied except the Chinese, who at that time were known to be exterminating the Chinese tiger as 'an impediment to pastoral and agricultural progress'. The reports, supplemented by what was known by the IUCN, were uniformly depressing.

According to my informants there were only 130 Siberian tigers, all of which were in the Sikhote-Alin region of the Soviet Far East. The number of surviving Chinese tigers could not be estimated. There were no accurate figures for the Indo-Chinese either, because several countries within its range were at war. The devastation caused by hostilities and particularly the widespread destruction of forests by the US Air Force using napalm and arsenical defoliants in Vietnam, represented a huge loss of habitat for tigers. There were, however, a few reports of their preying on dead or wounded soldiers, or attacking isolated sentries. Thailand, Malaya and eastern Burma were each reported to have 'several hundred' tigers. A tentative figure of 2000 was given for this race. For the Indian, the so-called Royal Bengal Tiger, figures were also vague. Mr K. S. Sankhala, at that time Director of the Delhi Zoological Park and an expert on tigers, thought the Indian population to be between 2000 and 3000. Bangladesh was believed to have about 150, Nepal a similar number, Bhutan 200 and western Burma a few. As the number of Indian tigers had been estimated at 40000 as recently as 1930, this new figure, totalling perhaps 3500, at least enabled a resolution to be passed at the IUCN Congress in

New Delhi to add the Indian race to the *Red Data Book* of endangered mammals. But when a detailed census was made in 1972, the figure for India had dropped again to only 1827. Everyone was shocked by this low figure.

The Caspian tiger, which used to occupy a range extending from eastern Turkey through northern Iran to Afghanistan and northward around the Caspian Sea to the shores of Lake Aral and Lake Balkash in the USSR, had disappeared except for a few reports of tracks seen in the Elburz mountains of Iran and on the banks of the Oxus in Afghanistan. Later investigation disproved these reports and the race must now be regarded as extinct. The Sumatran tiger was thought to number about 400, but later studies reduced this figure; as the rate of loss by poachers has remained at about 100 per annum, the future of this race is at least doubtful. The Javan race had been reduced to six or seven animals at the time of my investigation; now there are only four or five, all of which are in the Meru Betiri reserve. Such a number obviously does not represent a genetically viable breeding stock and this race is doomed. Finally, I was told that a few of the small Balinese tigers still survived, but when I visited Bali I found the race, like the Caspian, was extinct.

Thus, after a lengthy investigation, the position was that out of the eight races of the tiger two were already extinct, four were nearing extinction and only two, the Indian and the Indo-Chinese, looked like possible survivors if immediate action could be taken to save them. With Vietnam, Laos, Cambodia and Korea in the grip of military operations and Burma virtually closed to foreigners, this left only Peninsular Malaya and Thailand where effective action might be taken to save the Indo-Chinese tiger. The range of the Indian race, however, lay almost entirely within countries where co-operation was possible – India, Nepal, Bhutan and Bangladesh. Bhutan at that time was still closed to the outside world, as Nepal had been until the 1950s, but contact might be established. Speed of action was essential.

I prepared a paper for the World Wildlife Fund outlining my proposals. I wanted an all-out international effort to save the Indian tiger and to extend it to other surviving races if this proved possible. If we publicized the facts about the plight of what was probably the world's best known and most glamorous animal, I was confident that we could raise about a million dollars to help the governments in the countries concerned to create special tiger reserves. In addition, we should campaign for international legislation to ban tiger-hunting and the trade in tiger skins. There was little effective action we could take to limit the destruction of the tiger's forest habitat, but the creation of reserves would at least save some areas.

Perhaps I was rushing my fences. When my paper was considered at a joint meeting of the WWF and IUCN at our headquarters in Switzerland, it met stiff opposition. The WWF had insufficient funds for existing projects and it might take several years to raise the million dollars I needed. The IUCN wanted time to verify my population estimates. In spite of my impassioned pleas, the best I could get was a promise of 'further consideration'. I remained convinced that delay would be fatal to the tiger.

One of the arguments put forward against my proposals was that we did not know whether the governments concerned would be willing to co-operate. I decided to find out, making India my first stop.

Zafar Futehally, Vice President of the WWF organization in India, prepared for my visit by publishing half-page advertisements about the plight of the tiger, which were paid for by local benefactors. They paved the way for the series of meetings which he arranged for me. These included exploratory discussions with various officials, public lectures, broadcasts and press conferences. Everywhere I was encouraged to find a genuine interest in the possibility of saving the tiger from extinction.

During the week Charles de Haes, at that time acting as HRH Prince Bernhard's assistant on wildlife matters, arrived in New Delhi from Australia. His presence proved invaluable, as I was by then feeling the strain of the continuous succession of meetings in such a climate. He accom-

panied me to my first interview with Mrs Indira Gandhi, at
that time the formidable Prime Minister of India. I say formidable because I feel that anyone who holds this office as
successfully as she did must have an extraordinary constitu-
tion. However, when she received us in her dimly-lit and
soberly furnished room at Government House, her manner
was charming and conversation far from formal. She has the
innate poise and calm expression peculiar to most Indian
women, but also intellectual depths which few can match,
as many politicians have found to their cost.

Indira Gandhi's interest in wildlife is genuine. She
inherited from her father, Jawaharlal Nehru, an abiding
love for the beauties of nature which she has often expressed
and her garden is always occupied by various wild animal
pets. The tiger is to her an Indian symbol of national importance. Having seen me on television the previous night,
she was already familiar with the object of our visit. As a
matter of fact, she said, she had already instructed all state
governments to give the tiger maximum protection. Far
from questioning the proposals I put to her, she was quick to
accept them.

I explained that we could not hope to save all the tigers,
but that the wisest and most practical course would be to
create fully protected reserves for them in areas where
sufficient numbers survived to represent viable breeding
populations. Secondly, that really effective control of hunting
and of the highly organized poaching should be introduced.
And thirdly that legislation would be required to stop the
massive exportation of tiger skins to other countries. If the
Indian government could undertake these steps, I said, I
would arrange for a world-wide campaign through the
WWF, to raise the equivalent of one million dollars for
equipping the new reserves and sending experts to help set
up the management plans and the necessary research
projects. Charles, with the wisdom of his previous experience
in international affairs, was quick to interject that such a
programme could only succeed if directed and co-ordinated
by the highest authority.

'Very well,' said the Prime Minister, 'I shall form a special committee – a Tiger Task Force – which will report to me personally.'

A little stunned by the speed with which her decision had been made, I asked tentatively whether I might announce it at my press conference that evening.

'Certainly,' she said.

What was even more gratifying was that the Tiger Task Force was appointed the following day, under the chairmanship of one of India's most dynamic politicians, Dr Karan Singh, at that time Minister of Tourism and Civil Aviation and later Minister of Health and Family Planning. He drove the committee hard. Mr K. S. Sankhala was appointed as Director of what came to be called 'Project Tiger'; Zafar Futehally served as the essential link with the World Wildlife Fund. Field surveys were conducted and a list of reserves proposed. A six-year plan, involving the Indian government in the expenditure of more than £2 million was later approved by Parliament. Bearing in mind India's tremendous economic and social problems, this was a magnificent example to the rest of Asia.

Dr Karan Singh took the chair at my final meeting in New Delhi. In the course of a splendid speech he said, in an amusing aside, that as thousands of tigers had been shot in the days of the British Raj, it was appropriate that an Englishman should now be leading the crusade to save the species from extinction. I left India vastly encouraged, though guiltily aware that I had now committed the World Wildlife Fund to a million dollars – at that time nearly £400000.

Bangladesh was my next objective. I had explored this country during an expedition in 1967 and had found plenty of evidence of the famous Sunderbans tigers, which lived semi-aquatically in the enormous swamps at the mouths of the Ganges and Brahmaputra. I wanted a national park there to protect them. I knew this would be difficult, as Bangladesh was only just emerging from its devastating war with Pakistan.

When I got as far as Calcutta, all the commercial airline pilots came out on strike. At the best of times Calcutta is the last place I would choose in which to be grounded, but now every street was jammed with an influx of more than a million refugees from Bangladesh. No city in the world is more irredeemably horrible, nor fills me with such an over-powering combination of repugnance, compassion and futility. In a shade temperature of 105°F, I wandered around the blistering tarmac of Dum Dum airport to where a United Nations relief plane was about to take off for Dacca. The big blond Swedish pilot listened sympathetically to my story.

'Sure – jump in,' he said and I found myself the only passenger among seven tons of crated biscuits destined for the refugee camp at Dacca. No ticket, no formalities. It reminded me of my many hitch-hiked flights during the war. But it turned out to be a hair-raising journey. The monsoon was just breaking and the pilot flew at only a few hundred feet above ground to avoid the violent turbulence, which sent everything not lashed down flying about in the cabin. I was hit on the head by an air-borne thermos flask. To calm my nerves I counted the lightning flashes exploding from the boiling black clouds, which for a while were at a rate of thirty-one to the minute. I was thankful to land on the bomb-damaged runway at Dacca.

My old Bengali colleague, Mr G. M. M. Karim, met me at the still intact Intercontinental Hotel. He had been a member of my 1967 expedition, and was now Deputy Director of Tourism. Somehow he had salvaged the conservation plans which I had drafted when Bangladesh had been East Paki-stan, and he said these were being adopted by the new régime.

After a quick shower I accompanied Karim on a round of official visits. Not all my friends had survived the war. Those who had were in a state of euphoria about the re-construction of their ravaged country. I called on the new President, Justice Abu Syed Choudhury, a learned and delightful scholar who had no illusions about the problems

F

of the new nation, but nevertheless supported my wish to salvage what remained of its wildlife. Finally, late on the second evening, I was taken to see the Prime Minister, Sheikh Mujibur Rahman, the creator of Bangladesh, whose face was now familiar on television screens throughout the world.

He was a remarkable man, of super-abundant energy and regularly worked a sixteen-hour day. His small, heavily guarded office was in an overcrowded temporary building. The narrow stairway was jammed with jabbering petitioners. In the anteroom newspaper correspondents were playing with a leopard cub which someone wanted to present to the Prime Minister. Harassed clerks were darting in and out like distracted hens. The stifling atmosphere and the noise resembled a native bazaar.

The Prime Minister himself ushered me into his inner office. While we drank tea he listened to my proposals about the tiger and my offer of help from the World Wildlife Fund in creating a national park in the Sunderbans. He seemed delighted and from then on did most of the talking. His mood was confident and at times gay, in spite of the burden he carried. In his long black jacket, buttoned from throat to knee above white *pyjamas*, he looked much taller than photographs suggested and much fitter than when he had been released from captivity in Pakistan.

'Look,' he said, 'I've already put the tiger on our new currency – I'll put it on our postage stamps, too, and we'll make it our national animal! I've also forbidden the killing of wild animals and any further destruction of forests. Certainly we will have a national park in the Sunderbans – it will help to earn money from tourists, which we badly need. Let's have one at Pablakhali as well. There are lots of tigers there and we can protect them as soon as the Indian army has finished off the rebels.'

I did not have the heart to tell him that, having explored the Chittagong Hill Tracts around Pablakhali in 1967, I doubted that any tigers still survived there. His enthusiasm was so splendid that I let him talk on, which he did for nearly half an hour, his white teeth gleaming under his Edwardian moustache. Finally he glanced at his watch and said that his Cabinet was waiting for him and he must go. He shook my hand warmly and said we must meet again soon. I was captivated by his vivacious manner and little thought that he was destined later to fall to an assassin's bullets.

Until midnight I was busy with the press and recording a broadcast about the tiger. At seven next morning as I drove to the airport with Karim, I looked through the morning papers, all of which carried front-page stories of the Prime Minister's plans for the Sunderbans national park. It was a promising start.

Fortunately the Royal Nepalese Airline had a flight to Katmandu, my next destination. The approach to the world's only Hindu kingdom is always an exciting experience. After the hot plains of India, one weaves through the foothills above a mosaic of terraced fields of rice and millet towards the capital, with the extravagant panorama of the Himalayas stretched across the horizon. On the right is Everest and to the far left Annapurna. Katmandu itself is 4500 feet above sea level and the air was deliciously cool as I stepped from the plane. My old friends, John Blower and the brilliant American biologist George Schaller, were there to greet me. John was the FAO adviser on wildlife conservation to the Nepalese government. George, after his remarkable work on the snow leopard, was studying high-altitude sheep in the Himalayas.

On previous visits to Nepal I had met HM King Mahendra and Queen Ratna, who had later attended a WWF Congress in Geneva. Conservation in Nepal was making slow but steady progress, though there was still only one effective reserve, for the one-horned rhinoceroses at Chitawan. I wanted new reserves for the tiger, notably at Sukla Phanta and at Karnali, which was the best tiger area in the country, though unfortunately still listed as a 'royal hunting preserve'. Above all I wanted to see Mount Everest and the surrounding Khumbu area turned into a national park. King

Mahendra had promised his support for these proposals and thanks to John Blower they seemed likely to be approved. Then unfortunately the King had died. He had only recently been succeeded by HM King Birendra, to whom HRH Prince Bernhard, then President of the World Wildlife Fund, had given me an introduction. Nobody yet knew what the new king's policies would be and in Nepal matters of this kind depend on a decision from the throne.

While waiting for a call from the palace, I had time for meetings with the FAO and UNESCO representatives and with the British Ambassador, Sir Terence O'Brien, who was kind enough to invite me to dine at the embassy in order to meet Sir Edmund Hillary, just back from the Himalayas. I even had time for a quick visit to Chitawan and John Blower took me by light plane up to Mount Langtang, where we made a somewhat unorthodox landing at 12400 feet in a stony valley near some scampering yaks. It is impossible to be in Katmandu without enjoyment. Whichever way one turns in its narrow, crooked streets there are new vistas of temples, stupas and pagodas, more intricately carved gables, corbals and doors, more fluttering prayer-flags and spinning prayer-wheels, more glaring dragons and colourful demons. Even in the poorer outskirts there is more beauty than squalor, where the potters, wood-carvers, tinkers and other craftsmen sit at work in their doorways and the market women erect their pyramids of brightly coloured tropical fruits and vegetables.

I was entertained once more, as all visitors are, at the famous *Yak and Yeti*, a converted Rana palace owned by the almost legendary Boris, the White Russian adventurer. It was all very pleasant, but I was still without news from the palace. The King's personal secretary kept saying 'in a day or two', but finally confessed that as His Majesty was still in mourning and very busy with new government appointments, it would not be possible for him to see me that week. As I had an important meeting to attend in Switzerland, I could not wait that long.

Nevertheless, though my visit was badly timed, it bore

fruit. When Prince Bernhard later visited Nepal, considerable progress had been made. His Majesty had appointed
his brother, HRH Prince Gyanendra, to take charge of
conservation. The recommendations which John Blower and
I had previously made were speedily implemented. Not only
was Sukla Phanta gazetted as a protected reserve, but
Karnali also. As there were tigers at Chitawan, Nepal now
had three good tiger reserves. Even better news followed.
When Prince Gyanendra came to the next WWF Congress,
at Bonn, he announced that Mount Everest and the Khumbu
had become a national park. Scenically it is probably the
most important one in the world, in an area already being
badly damaged by the litter of trekking parties and the
constant lopping of trees for fuel. My wife and I visited it in
1972, having flown by helicopter up to the new Japanese
lodge above Thyangboche. From our window 11 300 feet
above sea level, the view of Everest, Lhotse, Nuptse and
Ama Dablam can only be described as stupendous.

To return to the tiger, my colleagues at the World Wildlife
Fund forgave me for having committed them to raise a
million dollars when they learned the extent to which India,
Bangladesh and Nepal were willing to co-operate. Prince
Bernhard formally launched what we called 'Operation
Tiger' in September 1972. It was the biggest international
effort we had yet attempted. As I had prophesied, the tiger
story proved irresistible to the press and broadcasters. Every-
body knew and admired this glamorous animal and was
appalled by the thought that it might disappear for ever.
Money poured in from country after country.

In England the famous artist, David Shepherd, painted a
superb portrait of a tiger, from which a limited edition of
signed reproductions were sold at a profit of £120000 for the
fund. I wrote a book about tigers to help the appeal and so
did K. S. Sankhala and Billy Arjan Singh in India. I lec-
tured and broadcasted about the appeal in six different
countries. The WWF sold tens of thousands of ties, ash-trays,
T-shirts and other items bearing the tiger symbol. Children
in the WWF Youth Service in Great Britain, Switzerland and

the Netherlands alone raised £300000. A group of children from seven countries was invited to India to see real wild tigers and was received by Indira Gandhi and fêted by the press and television. Within only eighteen months we had far exceeded our target figure – we had raised more than $1 700000.

Meanwhile, almost all the countries of Asia had banned tiger-hunting and the export of skins. Eighty-two of the world's airlines signed a pledge prepared by the WWF, agreeing not to promote hunting safaris concerned with endangered species such as the tiger. The final knell to the trade in tiger-skin coats was sounded when the Convention on International Trade in Endangered Species of Wild Fauna and Flora became international law. Women who still wore such coats found themselves being hissed in public. By then there were ten tiger reserves in India, three in Nepal, and one each in Bangladesh and Bhutan, all protecting the Indian race. Indonesia was doing its best to save the Sumatran and Javan races. Malaysia and Thailand had five reserves for the Indo-Chinese tiger. The USSR had improved the guarding of its Siberian tigers (which had increased to 150) and even China had put its remaining tigers under protection. India's efforts had been outstanding.

When Mr K. S. Sankhala presented a report, illustrated by his own superb colour photographs, at the 1976 WWF Congress in San Francisco, he was given a standing ovation. The tiger was saved, he said, and numbers had already increased substantially in the Indian reserves. All forms of endangered Indian wildlife, such as the gaur, the barasingha, the four-horned antelope, the crocodile, the clouded leopard and the pygmy hog, were also benefiting from the strict protection and scientific management given to the reserves. By this time the WWF had supplied $815000-worth of anti-poaching vehicles, motor-launches, two-way radio sets, binoculars, uniforms and other equipment for wardens in the six countries involved. 'Operation Tiger' had, in fact, been one of our greatest successes.

13

THE TASK AHEAD

THE success stories described in this book were chosen to show that progress is being made in the conservation of wildlife. It would, however, be idle to pretend that all the many endangered animals of the world can be similarly saved. Time is running out for too many of them. Some, which now have such small and scattered populations that reproduction has become a matter of mere chance encounter, will disappear before help can reach them. Others will be wiped out by introduced predators, or by the destruction of their habitats. Many little-known animals and many of the 20000 endangered plant species will be totally destroyed by the felling and burning of tropical rain-forests, which is still continuing at a combined rate of fifty acres per minute in south-east Asia, Africa and South America. But the fundamental threat to all wildlife and indeed to all life on earth is, of course, the combination of the human population explosion and the unbridled excesses of modern technology. The technological gigantism which now enables man literally to move mountains, or to destroy the rain-forests on such a massive scale, shows our failure to recognize that we are still almost totally mismanaging our planet and its life-support systems. What is happening to wildlife and the habitats of all wild creatures is the explicit writing on the wall for our own survival.

Some species have the dice so heavily loaded against them that no amount of care and protection seems likely to prevent their eventual disappearance. An example is the California condor, a truly magnificent bird with a wing-span of nearly ten feet. Its great size and the fact that it is a carrion-eater likely to be seen on the carcasses of domestic livestock, make it extremely vulnerable to any farmer with a gun. Its feeding range extends for fifty miles and during these flights it is very liable to pick up rodents killed by pesticides. It has an extremely slow natural reproductive rate, for it does not breed until six years old and then lays only one egg every other year. In consequence, though given maximum protection in the Los Padres National Forest, its main refuge, three adults are still lost every year for every two young ones raised to maturity. Inevitably, its population is steadily declining and only forty are now left. Though there will be many more conservation successes, there will also be inevitable failures which may never be able to be made good.

The IUCN maintains in its famous *Red Data Books* an accurate record of all the mammals, birds, reptiles, amphibia and fishes of the world which are known to be in danger. Further volumes on invertebrates and plants are currently being compiled. The immensity of the task facing conservationists can be judged by examining them. They are gold-mines of detailed and fascinating information. Every species is classified in categories decided by experts in the Survival Service Commission. The first category, appropriately printed on red sheets, is 'endangered', meaning that numbers have been reduced to a critically low level, or that the habitat is so drastically damaged that the species is in imminent danger of extinction. The second is 'vulnerable', where populations are known to be decreasing, or are under the threat of such serious factors that the species seems likely to move into the first category. The third is 'rare', where the population is very small and at risk, though its survival is not yet actually endangered. There is another category for species suspected of belonging to one of the other three, but for which insufficient information is yet available. The data sheets are constantly monitored and revised, so that conservation action can be modified or accelerated. Throughout the world the *Red Data Books* form the solid basis on which the protection of wildlife is planned.

The number of mammal species thus listed is at present 294 and the number of birds 345. Even among some of the large and well-known animals which are included, such as the beautiful snow leopard, the protective arm of conservation may be unable to reach them before it is too late. *The Red Book* shows why. The snow leopard has a range extending from the Russian Pamirs and the Himalayas to Tian Shan and the Altai Range. It is heavily persecuted throughout this entire region for the value of its magnificent fur and because it preys occasionally on domestic animals which often graze up to the snow line. Although officially a protected species in several countries where it occurs, there seems little hope that the mountain tribesmen can be prevented from shooting it so long as the black market continues to pay high prices for its skin.

The little musk deer, which occupies similarly remote mountainous regions, is another animal which is very difficult to protect. It has legal protection in China, Nepal, Bhutan, India and Pakistan, but the export of the musk pods of the male still continues at a rate of tens of thousands a year for the benefit of traditional Asian medicine and the perfume trade. There is no control over its slaughter in southern Tibet or Burma, or in the many parts of its range under military jurisdiction. As the sexes are difficult to distinguish at normal hunting distance, thousands of females are uselessly killed. The musk deer could probably be farmed if the perfume trade cannot be induced to use a synthetic substitute for musk entirely instead of partially, but if this trade and the Asian medicinal trade continue, the species is likely to be eventually exterminated. There are unfortunately several other examples where conservation seems at present powerless to intervene effectively. The only practical solution is to attempt to create fully protected reserves in areas where such species breed and where full co-operation is obtainable from the local governments concerned. This the World Wildlife Fund is trying to do.

Hungry nomadic people, such as those living in the harsh environment of the highlands of central Asia, must shoot or trap wild animals in order to stay alive and to clothe themselves against the bitter winter climate. On the other hand, in the abundance of the jungles of south-east Asia, the Amazon basin and New Guinea, the native tribes live in equilibrium with nature, destroying little except for their immediate frugal needs. Neither food nor clothing is a problem. In such regions conservation difficulties are almost entirely concerned with unwise government land-use policies. In order to obtain quick cash returns in foreign currencies, mineral rights and forests are leased to foreign companies. The exploitation of marine resources, such as the harvesting of whales, fur seals, turtles and fish, particularly in South American waters, is also largely in foreign hands. This inequitable use of declining natural resources for the benefit of richer nations can only make the acceptance of wise conservation measures by the Third World more difficult to obtain.

Analysis of the endangered birds listed in the *Red Data Books* shows a very high proportion – more than half – inhabiting small islands. Many of these have extremely small populations. The Mauritius kestrel, for example, was reduced to only seven or eight birds. In such cases a possible chance for survival lies in an attempt to catch a pair and breed them in captivity and this is now being tried on Mauritius. In addition, this unique bird's small remaining habitat has been put under protection and the monkeys which prey on its eggs are being controlled. Thanks to these measures, two wild pairs succeeded in producing five flying young in 1977, thus raising the world population of the species to thirteen. So there is still a slender chance of recovery, even on an island so badly exploited as this one has been.

Where governments are sufficiently enlightened and co-operative, some quite astonishing results can often be achieved. One such notable example occurred in Australia. An obscure little bird known as the noisy scrub-bird, which was thought to have become extinct in 1889, was re-discovered in an area near the city of Perth. HRH Prince Philip, President of the British branch of the World Wildlife Fund, happened to be visiting Australia at the time and showed great interest in the discovery. Learning that the area where the colony of noisy scrub-birds was located had been scheduled for building a new town, he urged that the plan should be modified. To the lasting credit of the West Australian state government, it was agreed to build the town elsewhere and to put the habitat of the birds under immediate protection. The birds responded to this generosity by multiplying and the species has now been saved from almost certain extinction.

Public interest is a vital factor in saving wildlife and perhaps particularly so in respect to birds. The strength of public opinion in favour of the osprey in Scotland is demonstrated by the fact that a quarter of a million people pay every year for the privilege of seeing one at the Loch Garten reserve, which was created for ospreys by the Royal Society for the Protection of Birds. In Turkey, it was public interest which helped the survival of the thirty-four waldrapps (bald ibises) which nest only on a cliff in the small town of Bireçek, on the upper Euphrates. A similar nationalistic pride protects the ultra-rare Japanese crested ibis, only about ten of which are thought to exist on the island of Sado and the Noto Peninsula, where they are regarded as national treasures. Probably no rare bird in the world has received more constant publicity or public support than the whooping crane of North America. It is closely guarded, filmed, photographed and discussed in the press from its breeding grounds in the Wood Buffalo National Park in Canada to its winter quarters on the Gulf coast of Texas. The patient skill and co-operation of Canadian and American wildlife experts enabled its population to creep up slowly from 33 in 1959 to 126 in 1977, in spite of a poor rate of breeding success and occasional losses to trigger-happy hunters during its long migration across the prairies.

Another imaginative project supported by the WWF which

is showing great promise is the restoration of the peregrine falcon in the United States. Both in North America and in Europe this fine bird has been one of the worst sufferers from DDT pesticides, the poisons causing high direct mortality among adults and widespread breeding failures. Unfortunately the peregrine is also in constant demand by falconers of every country and many Arab sheikhs are willing to pay as much as £2000 for one. Dr Tom Cade of the Cornell University Laboratory of Ornithology has now perfected a method of breeding the species under laboratory conditions and then placing the nestlings in groups of three to six in artificially constructed nest sites, where they are fed and guarded until able to fly and catch their own food. In the language of falconry he is 'hacking young birds back to the wild'. In spite of a few early losses, the experiment is increasingly successful, some fifty-five captive-bred birds having already been released at traditional cliff-nesting sites in seven states. A second venture is being tested in Colorado, where captive-bred nestlings are placed in the nests of wild peregrines whose eggs have failed to hatch. They have been readily accepted and reared to maturity. There is now substantial hope that the American peregrine may recover from the appalling losses it suffered from DDT and kindred poisons.

The problems of conservation will increase in direct ratio to the continuing rise in the human population. The funds available from the United Nations, governments, foundations and voluntary sources are pitifully small. Even if the amount raised by the World Wildlife Fund were doubled, it could not keep pace with the demands for aid which pour in from all parts of the world. Priorities have to be set and maintained, even when this inevitably means that many deserving projects cannot be implemented. There are, however, encouraging signs of an emerging global conscience in matters of conservation. One such indication was the Saudi Arabian government's proposal of a one cent levy per barrel of oil to support the United Nations Environment Programme. If all the oil-producing countries agreed to this, it would provide an annual fund of 200 to 300 million dollars. The resolution was referred to the Secretary-General of the UN, Dr Kurt Waldheim, and it will be interesting to see what response it gains.

In the early days of the IUCN and WWF co-operative effort, the emphasis was on what might be termed 'fire-brigade' action. As each conservation emergency was identified, action was taken to overcome it. There will always be such emergencies. But as time passed it became increasingly clear that prevention was better than cure – and less costly also. The IUCN therefore began planning on a long-range basis, aimed at identifying problems before they assumed unmanageable proportions. Once the limiting factors were clearly seen, they could usually be attacked effectively. From this philosophy emerged an orderly, phased progression of activities on which priorities could be planned within the scientific and financial resources likely to be available. Areas containing representative samples or exceptional communities of animals, plants or habitats were first identified. A conservation strategy striking a realistic balance between urgency and practicability was then defined and this was closely co-ordinated with the work of the related United Nations agencies such as FAO, UNEP, and UNESCO, which with the IUCN now form what is termed the Ecosystem Conservation Group. The funds and the talent available world-wide for conservation are therefore now being employed on a much more rational and effective basis, with minimal risk of duplication of effort. Moreover, by encouraging co-operation and participation by governments on a regional basis within this overall strategy, an increasingly important 'multiplier-effect' is being achieved. The WWF has concentrated its public-awareness and fund-raising efforts in support of this strategy, notable recent examples being its global campaigns concerned with rain-forests and with marine life. These have resulted in the creation of a large number of representative sample areas being set aside as protected reserves before the impending threat of destruction could reach them. It is now clear that a concentration of preventive effort directed at a region or topic for a period of two or three years produces a more successful and lasting result than scattered 'fire-brigade' action.

The ultimate key to success will lie with education. It is not sheer perversity, but lack of knowledge of ecological principles which leads governments to take decisions ultimately harmful to the natural environment, or engineers to declare that building a dam will not upset the entire ecosystem of the valleys below. Again and again reassurances based on ignorance have been blandly given and as readily accepted by governments. One frequently hears leading statesmen and politicians quoting admirable maxims about conservation; but ask yourself how many of them have done more than pay lip service to the cause in order to placate an anxious electorate? They are lamentably few, because most politicians do not understand the technicalities of the problems.

The big companies in Japan, Europe and North America, which are destroying the tropical forests of the Third World, are woefully ignorant of the ultimate harm they are doing to science, to medicine, to plant breeders and to the wildlife of the richest genetic resource on earth. I am not suggesting that timber is not needed for industry, or that dams should not be built, but that what is needed is more education and a far closer co-operation between qualified conservationists, governments, engineers and industry. Dam building, mineral extraction and the exploitation of forest trees should be planned on sound ecological lines, to minimize the harmful consequences and to ensure the survival and regeneration of renewable natural resources. The knowledge and the techniques required are freely available and are of proven effectiveness. Only education can create the willingness to use them.

In a Utopian world, every politician would be obliged to read *Ecological Principles for Economic Development* before being allowed to take his seat in the legislature. This book, which originated from a conference on the ecological aspects of international development, was produced at the suggestion of my friend Max Nicholson. He was at that time Convenor of the International Biological Programme, after many years of experience in advising governments about land-use policies. The authors were also leading experts: Raymond Dasmann, John Milton and Peter Freeman. They demonstrated, by means of factual case histories, the paramount need for an understanding of economic, social and environmental realities if human suffering and serious environmental damage were to be avoided. Moreover, the book provided clear guide-lines which, if followed, could protect renewable natural resources and revolutionize the task of conservationists. Unfortunately, there is no means of obliging decision-makers or politicians to read it, though it has been widely distributed by the IUCN.

To the hungry millions in the Third World, the concept of protecting wildlife will continue to be regarded as inexplicable, or as a white man's fantasy, until such time as famine is conquered. The traditions among primitive people mentioned in this book, which condemn them to live at bare subsistence level and which turn potentially productive land into desert, will not change until we learn that it is better to export knowledge and practical guidance than merely to export our surplus grain to the starving. Only with a full belly and regained self-respect can a poor man be expected to raise his eyes from the ground and learn to appreciate the wonders of nature around him.

Meanwhile, those of us whose lives do not depend on the chance discovery of sufficient food to survive for another day in a hostile wilderness, must continue our efforts to protect the natural world. We must learn to recognize that each unique animal species which disappears for ever was part of the same evolutionary process to which we ourselves belong. That each additional loss is not merely a loss to our natural heritage, but a further weakening of man's own tenure on earth. Even if we are loth to peer too far into the future, we must at least try to make sure that our children's children will not wonder why we did not try hard enough to save the birds and beasts and flowers for them to enjoy.

The people whose work I have described in this book have demonstrated that further losses are not always inevitable. Some of them gave their services voluntarily in achieving their successes. But even if one were to add up the total cost of the work and travel of all the dozen individuals chiefly concerned, it would still amount to little more than the price of one of the giant bulldozers which are now destroying the rain-forests. After all, conservation is really a matter of getting our priorities right. The technology which produced the giant bulldozer has conferred many obvious benefits on mankind. It is, perhaps, reassuring to know that non-stick saucepans were a direct outcome of sending rockets to the moon. But to the man in the street who worries about the quality of life for his grandchildren, the priority given to the expenditure of billions on this adventurous technological exercise may seem questionable. I am sufficient of an optimist to believe the time will come when even politicians will agree that the protection of our natural environment should come first.

Appendix

Scientific names of mammals, birds and reptiles mentioned in the text

MAMMALS

Alpaca   *Lama pacos*
Antelope, Four-horned   *Tetracerus quadricornis*
Barasingha   *Cervus duvauceli*
Bat, Fox   *Pteropus giganteus*
    Orange-breasted Fox   *Pteropus seychellensis*
Bear, Polar   *Thalarctos maritimus*
    Sloth   *Melursus ursinus*
    Sun   *Helarctos malayanus*
Beaver   *Castor fiber*
Blackbuck   *Antilope cervicapra*
Boar, Wild   *Sus scrofa cristatus*
Buffalo, Asiatic   *Bubalus bubalis*
Cat, Leopard   *Felis bengalensis*
    Pampas   *Felis colocolo*
Chimpanzee   *Pan troglodytes*
Chinchilla   *Chinchilla brevicaudata*
Civet   *Viverricula indica*
Deer, Chital   *Axis axis*
    Hog   *Axis porcinus*
    Mouse   *Tragulus javanicus*
    Musk   *Moschus moschiferus*
    Père David's   *Elaphurus davidianus*
    Sambar   *Cervus unicolor*

Dolphin, Gangetic *Platanista gangetica*
Dugong *Dugong dugon*
Elephant, African *Loxodonta africana*
    Indian *Elaphus maximus*
Fox *Vulpes vulpes*
Gazelle, Chinkara *Gazella gazella*
  Rhim *Gazella leptoceros*
Gemsbok *Oryx gazella*
Gibbon, Siamang *Hylobates syndactylus*
Gorilla *Gorilla gorilla*
Guanaco *Lama guanicoe*
Hartebeeste, Jackson's *Alcelaphus buselaphus jacksoni*
Hog, Pygmy *Porcula sylvania*
Hyena *Hyaena hyaena*
Jackal *Canis aureus*
Jaguar *Panthera onca*
Langur *Presbytis entellus*
Leopard *Panthera pardus*
    Clouded *Neofelis nebulosa*
    Snow *Panthera uncia*
Lion, African *Panthera leo*
    Asiatic *Panthera leo persica*
Llama *Lama glama*
Mongoose *Herpestes edwardsi*
Nilgai *Boselaphus tragocamelus*
Ocelot *Felis pardalis*
Orang-utan *Pongo pygmaeus*
Oryx, Arabian *Oryx leucoryx*
    Beisa *Oryx gazella beisa*
    Scimitar-horned *Oryx tao*
Panda, Giant *Ailuropoda melanoleuca*
    Red *Ailurus fulgens*
Porcupine, American *Erethizon dorsatum*
    Indian *Hystrix indica*
    Indonesian *Thecurus sp.*
Rhesus Monkey *Macaca mulatta*
Rhinoceros, Black *Diceros bicornis*
    Indian *Rhinoceros unicornis*
    Javan *Rhinoceros sondaicus*
    Sumatran *Didermocerus sumatrensis*
    White *Ceratotherium simum*

Seal, Galápagos Fur   *Arctocephalus galapagoensis*
Sealion, Galápagos   *Zalophus californianus*
Tiger, Balinese   *Panthera tigris balica*
    Caspian   *Panthera tigris virgata*
    Chinese   *Panthera tigris amoyensis*
    Indian   *Panthera tigris tigris*
    Indo-Chinese   *Panthera tigris corbetti*
    Javan   *Panthera tigris sondaica*
    Siberian   *Panthera tigris altaica*
    Sumatran   *Panthera tigris sumatrae*
Vicuña   *Vicugna vicugna*
Whale, Blue   *Balaenoptera musculus*
    Fin   *Balaenoptera physalus*
    Humpback   *Megaptera novaeangliae*
    Sperm   *Physeter catodon*
Wildebeeste   *Connochaetes taurinus*
Wolf   *Canis lupus*
Yak   *Bos grunniens*
Zebra   *Equus burchelli*

BIRDS

Albatross, Galápagos Waved   *Diomedea irrorata*
Booby, Abbot's   *Sula abbotti*
    Red-footed   *Sula sula rubripes*
Brush Warbler, Aldabra   *Bebrornis aldabranus*
    Seychelles   *Bebrornis seychellensis*
Condor, Andean   *Vultur gryphus*
    California   *Gymnogyps californianus*
Cormorant, Galápagos Flightless   *Nannopterum harrisi*
Coucal, Aldabra   *Centropus toulou insularis*
Crane, Whooping   *Grus americana*
Diver, Great Northern   *Gavia immer*
Dove, Aldabra Turtle   *Streptopelia picturata coppingeri*
    Barred Ground   *Geopelia striata*
    Cousin Turtle   *Streptopelia picturata rostrata*
    Galápagos   *Zenaida galapagoensis*
Drongo, Aldabra   *Dicrurus aldabranus*
Falcon, Peregrine   *Falco peregrinus*
Finches, Galápagos   *Geospiza* sp., *Camarhynchus* sp., etc.

Flamingo, Aldabra   *Phoenicopterus ruber roseus*
Flycatcher, Large-billed   *Myiarchus magnirostris*
   Seychelles Paradise   *Tchitrea corvina*
Fody, Aldabra *Foudia eminentissima aldabrana*
   Madagascar   *Foudia Madagascariensis*
Frigatebirds   *Fregata* sp.
Goose, Barnacle   *Branta leucopsis*
   Brent   *Branta bernicla*
   Canada   *Branta canadensis*
   Néné   *Branta sandvicensis*
Grebe, Giant Pied-billed   *Podilymbus gigas*
   Great Crested   *Podiceps cristatus*
   Pied-billed   *Podilymbus podiceps*
   Puna   *Podiceps taczanowskii*
   Short-winged   *Centropelma micropterum*
Gull, Lava   *Larus fuliginosus*
   Swallowtailed   *Creagrus furcatus*
Hawk, Galápagos   *Buteo galapagoensis*
Heron, Lava   *Butorides sundevalli*
   Little Green   *Butorides striatus*
Honeycreepers   *Drepanidinae* sp.
Ibis, Bald   *Geronticus eremita*
   Japanese Crested   *Nipponia nippon*
   Sacred   *Threskiornis aethiopica*
Kestrel, Aldabra   *Falco newtoni aldabrana*
   Mauritius   *Falco punctatus*
   Seychelles   *Falco araea*
Magpie Robin, Seychelles   *Copsychus seychellarum*
Martin, Galápagos   *Progne modesta*
Mockingbirds, Galápagos   *Nesomimus* sp.
Mynah, Indian   *Acridotheres tristis*
Nightjar, Jungle   *Caprimulgus indicus*
Osprey   *Pandion haliaetus*
Owl, Bare-legged Scops   *Otis insularis*
   Forest Eagle   *Bubo nipalensis*
Oxpecker, Red-billed   *Buphagus erythorhynchus*
Parrot, Seychelles Black   *Coracopsis nigra barklyi*
Peafowl   *Pavo cristatus*
Penguin, Galápagos   *Spheniscus mendiculus*
Pigeon, Aldabra Blue   *Alectroenas sganzine minor*
Plover, Crab   *Dromas ardeola*

Quetzal *Pharomachrus moccino*
Rail, Aldabra *Dryolimnas cuvieri aldabrana*
  Galápagos *Laterallus spilonotus*
Scrub-bird, Noisy *Atrichornis clamosus*
Shearwater, Audubon's *Puffinus l'herminieri*
  Wedge-tailed *Puffinus pacificus*
Sunbird, Aldabra *Nectarinia souimanga aldabrensis*
  Seychelles *Nectarinia dussumieri*
Tern, Bridled *Sterna anaethetus*
  Crested *Thalasseus bergii*
  Fairy *Gypsis alba*
  Lesser Noddy *Anous stolidus*
  Noddy *Anous stolidus*
  Sooty *Sterna fuscata*
Tropicbird, Red-tailed *Phaethon rubricauda*
  White-tailed *Phaethon lepturus*
White-eye, Aldabra *Zosterops maderaspatana aldabrensis*
  Japanese *Zosterops palpebrosa*

REPTILES

Chameleon, Tiger *Chamilio tigris*
Cobra *Naja naja*
Crocodile, Estuarine *Crocodilus porosus*
  Marsh *Crocodilus palustris*
  Nile *Crocodilus niloticus*
Geckos *Gekko* sp.
Gharial *Gavialis gangeticus*
Iguana, Galápagos Land *Conolophus subcristatus*
  Galápagos Marine *Amblyrhynchus cristatus*
Krait *Bungarus caeruleus*
Lizard, Galápagos Lava *Tropidurus* sp.
  Monitor *Varanus* sp.
Python *Python* sp.
Skinks *Chalcides* sp.
Tortoise, Galápagos Giant *Geochelone elephantopus*
  Indian Ocean Giant *Geochelone gigantea*
Turtle, Green *Chelonia mydas*
  Hawksbill *Eretmochelys imbricata*

Selected bibliography

Anon, *Project Tiger*, Indian Board for Wildlife, New Delhi, 1972.

Beamish, Tony, *Aldabra Alone*, Allen & Unwin, London, 1970.

Boswall, Jeffery, 'The Vicuña in Argentina', *Oryx*, XI: 448–53, 1972.

Carson, Rachel, *Silent Spring*, Houghton Mifflin, Boston, 1962.

Dasmann, Raymond, Milton, John, Freeman, Peter, *Ecological Principles for Economic Development*, International Union for Conservation of Nature, Morges, 1973.

Diamond, A. W., *Cousin Island, Seychelles*, International Council for Bird Preservation, 1975.

Eibl-Eibesfeldt, I., *Galápagos*, Charles Darwin Foundation, Brussels, 1960.

Fisher, J., Simon, N., Vincent, J., *The Red Book, Animals in Danger*, Collins, London, 1969.

Fitter, Richard, *Vanishing Animals of the World*, Midland Bank Ltd, London, 1968.

Gaymer, Roger, 'Aldabra – The Case for Conserving this Coral Atoll', *Oryx*, VIII: 348–52, 1966.

Goodwin, H. A., Holloway, C. W., *Red Data Book – Mammalia*, International Union for Conservation of Nature, Morges, 1972 *et seq.*

Government of Gujarat State, *The Gir Lion Sanctuary*, Gujarat, 1972.

Greenway, James C., *Extinct and Vanishing Birds of the World*, American Committee for International Wildlife Protection, New York, 1958.

Grimwood, I. R., 'Operation Oryx', *Oryx*, VI: 308–34, 1963; 'Operation Oryx: the Second Stage', *Oryx*, VII: 223–5, 1964.

Harrisson, Barbara, *Orang-utan*, Collins, London, 1962.
Henderson, D. S., 'Were they the last Arabian Oryx?', *Oryx*, XII: 347–50, 1974.
Jackson, Peter, 'Wildlife Man of the Year – Arjan Singh', *Wildlife '76*, 10–13, 1976.
Johnson, Peter, 'White Rhinoceros', *Wildlife '76*, 24–31, 1976.
Joslin, P., *Conserving the Asiatic Lion*, Proceedings, International Union for Conservation of Nature, 11: 24–33, 1973.
Jungius, H. 'Bolivia and the Vicuña', *Oryx*, XI: 325–46, 1972.
Kinloch, Bruce, *The Shamba Raiders*, Collins, London, 1972.
Koford, Carl B., 'The Vicuña and the Puna', *Ecological Monthly*, 27: 153–219, 1957.
La Bastille, Anne, 'How Fares the Poc?', *Audubon Magazine*, 74: 36–43, 1972; 'Ecology and Management of the Atitlán Grebe', *Wildlife Monograph*, 37: 1–66, 1974.
Lack, David, *Darwin's Finches*, Cambridge University Press, Cambridge, 1947.
Lionnet, Guy, *The Seychelles*, David & Charles, Newton Abbott, 1972.
Lord, John, *The Maharajahs*, Hutchinson, London, 1972.
MacKinnon, John, *In Search of the Red Ape*, Collins, London, 1974.
Moorhead, Alan, *Darwin and the Beagle*, Hamish Hamilton, London, 1969.
Morris, Desmond, *The Mammals*, Hodder & Stoughton, London, 1964.
Mountfort, Guy, *The Vanishing Jungle*, Collins, London, 1969; *Tigers*, David & Charles, Newton Abbott, 1973; 'International Efforts to Save the Tiger', *Biological Conservation*, 6: 48–52, 1974; *So Small a World*, Hutchinson, London, 1974.
Nelson, Bryan, *Galápagos, Island of Birds*, Longman, London, 1968.
Penny, Malcolm, *Birds of the Seychelles and Outlying Islands*, Collins, London, 1974; 'Western Indian Ocean', *Wildlife '76*, 114–21, 1976.
Sankhala, Kailash, *Tiger*, World Wildlife Fund, Zurich, 1974.
Schenkel, R., and Schenkel-Hulliger, L., *The Javan Rhinoceros in Udjung Kulon Nature Reserve*, Zoologisches Institut Universität, Basel, 1969.
Simon, Noel, Géroudet, Paul, *Last Survivors*, Patrick Stephens, London, 1970.

Singh, Arjan, *Tiger Haven*, Macmillan, London, 1973.

Soliman, S. M., *White Arabian Oryx*, Faculty of Education, Doha, Qatar, 1976.

Talbot, L. M., *A Look at Threatened Species*, International Union for Conservation of Nature, Morges, 1960.

Vincent, J., *Red Data Book – Aves*, International Union for Conservation of Nature, Morges, 1966 *et seq.*

Index